To Walt Mison
With thanks for the
Musical Experiences —
Bob Dotten
1988

Merle Evans—*Maestro of the Circus*

Merle Evans

Gene Plowden

MERLE EVANS
Maestro of the Circus

E. A. Seemann Publishing, Inc.
Miami, Florida

Copyright © 1971 by Gene Plowden

Library of Congress Catalog Card Number: 71-171867

ISBN 0-912458-04-6

All rights reserved including rights of reproduction and use in any form or by any means, including the making of copies by any photo process, or by any electronic or mechanical device, printed or written or oral, or recording for sound or visual reproduction or for use in any knowledge or retrieval system or device, unless permission is obtained from the copyright proprietors.

Manufactured in the United States of America

To my wife

DORIS

whose patience and understanding made this book possible.

Contents

Preface
1. Come to the Circus / *15*
2. Boy with a Horn / *19*
3. Showboat Down the Mississippi / *25*
4. Gabriel Blows his Horn / *33*
5. Life on the 101 Ranch / *40*
6. To the Top of the Mountain / *46*
7. In the Garden / *53*
8. No Smooth Sailing / *57*
9. Music for the Circus / *64*
10. The Grandest Show on Earth / *73*
11. Two Brothers Ringling / *79*
12. Ups and Downs on the Big Show / *86*
13. The Strange People / *91*
14. Band Leader and the Animals / *96*
15. Trouping in Foreign Lands / *101*
16. Ringling, Gumpertz and Petrillo / *108*
17. To College and Back / *113*
18. The Troubles of Troupers / *120*
19. Years of Change and Decline / *127*
20. Never Play that Again / *132*
21. Country Boy from Kansas / *139*
22. Bandmaster in Retirement / *144*
Epilogue / *153*

Illustrations

1 Frontispiece / 2
2. Merle Evans with the S. W. Brundage Carnival in 1909 / 27
3 Merle Evans with the S. W. Brundage Shows / 31
4 With National Stock Company band in 1910 / 34
5 With Murphy's Comedians' band in 1911 / 36
6 On tour with Armetta & Pullen Comedians in 1912 / 37
7 With the Buffalo Bill-101 Ranch Wild West Show in 1916 / 41
8 Buffalo Bill-101 Ranch Wild West Show band in 1917 / 44
9 Letter of instructions from Ringling to his new band leader / 49
10 Merle Evans in 1919 in Madison Square Garden / 52
11 Three circus notables of the 1920s / 59
12 Typical crowd under the Big Top in the 1920s / 61
13 Typical cue sheet used by Merle Evans / 66-67
14 The big Liberty bandwagon / 76
15 Merle Evans and his band under the Big Top in 1939 / 87
16 Uniforms for the 1940 season featured long coats and caps with floppy tops / 87
17 Two of the circus' greatest press agents at work / 88
18 Merle Evans as director of the Hardin Simmons University band in 1942 / 114
19 James Fraser drawing celebrating Merle Evans's return as circus band director in 1943 / 116
20, 21 Lauritz Melchior, the famous tenor, tries his hand at directing the circus band in 1944 (above), and tests his lung power on Merle Evans's cornet (below) / 117
22 Saints & Sinners citation of 1944 / 125

23 Evans and his band in 1946 / *126*
24 Merle Evans' band, gaudily uniformed, in 1955 / *129*
25 Arthur M. Concello, / *131*
26 Merle Evans Ring No. 32, Circus Model Builders / *141*
27 The cornet was his trademark / *134*
28 Changing times have reduced circus band to less than two dozen (1968) / *137*
29 Nena and Merle Evans / *147*

Preface

Merle Evans is one of the most remarkable men in the history of music in America. Born in the small town of Columbus, Kansas, he loved music, played cornet, and led bands in a variety of entertainment ventures before being hired as band director on the Ringling Bros. and Barnum & Bailey Combined Shows in 1919.

He retired at the end of the 1969 season. Still vigorous and in excellent health, he now devotes his time to making recordings, playing for Shrine circuses, teaching music, and leading high school and college bands throughout the nation.

Having known Merle Evans and admired his circus music for nearly forty years, I telephoned him at his home in Sarasota, Florida, to congratulate him on his retirement after sixty happy years as a trouper.

During our conversaion, I mentioned there ought to be a book written on his life. His reply was, "You're the only man I know qualified to write it." And that's how this book came to be.

Special thanks go to Merle and his wife, Nena, who gave such fine cooperation; to Arthur M. Concello, Jimmy Gardner, Gene Russell, Freddie Daw, and numerous other circus authorities who provided needed information and helped complete the project.

GENE PLOWDEN

Miami, Florida
November, 1971

Merle Evans—*Maestro of the Circus*

1

Come to the Circus

"Ladeez and Gentlemen, Children of all Ages---Welcome to the 1969 edition of 'The Greatest Show on Earth! ' "

The tall, blond, and handsome Harold Ronk, the singing ringmaster has swung into action, smiled and lifted the microphone to his chest as he had for twenty years to make the announcement. He added with a flourish, "And now it's Tally Ho and Away we go! "

The flags unfurled, there was a crashing, crescending blare of horns and roll of drums as hundreds of performers, brilliant in new costumes with glittering spangles from head to foot, swept into the vast arena, dancing and skipping and trotting to the music of Merle Evans and his band as performers before them had done for fifty happy and exciting seasons.

Merle, who had never missed or been late for a single performance in all that time, had assembled the finest circus musicians in the land. He stood proud and ramrod-straight on the podium, his back to the band and his eyes on the arena so that in one split second he could change tempo to accompany the performing horses, elephants, ferocious lions, tigers, and panthers in their breath-taking acts, or calm humans and animals in event of unexpected tragedy.

The program had promised "this prestigious prelude: Preceding the performance for the Pleasure of its Patrons, the Greatest Show on Earth Proudly Presents a Scintillating Siege of Silly Surprises and a Mood-Setting Medley of Tanbark Tunes, Performed on Ringling Bros. and Barnum & Bailey's Celebrated Concert Calliope," and there it was, wringing tears from men and women who remembered the circus "way back when."

The capital letters are the circus' own, of course, for everything about the grand old show, even in its 99th consecutive season, was hailed as "Bigger and Better than Ever!"

The theme this time is "Riding High", and here celebrated circus stars from around the globe combine with the most glittering panoply of pageantry that the world has ever known.

The program says thousands of miles were traveled, thousands of hours spent auditioning the myriad of wonders that will unfold in three marvelous, magical rings of the Greatest Show on Earth this night.

Merle Evans and his fellow "windjammers" will provide music for what it tells us will be "Fantastic Feats of Rarely Realized Horsemanship," for a "Noisy, Nervy Serenade of Athletes and Acrobats, Fumblers and Funnymen," then quickly switch to proper tempos for "Three Thrilling Rings of Juggling Juggernauts, Crowding the Air with a Galaxy of Glittering Globes and Granting Gravity a Halcyon Holiday."

Here come the clowns "in a tidal wave of terrific tomfoolery, featuring an agile assortment of madcap merrymen with a bountiful bagful of stupefying stunts, followed by talented tacticians of tumbling, twisting and turning who taunt terrible tragedy at every turn."

Then "an alp-high avalanche of high-wire histrionics and harrowingly heady hilarity, astoundingly agile artists in an amazing amalgamation of ambitious acrobatic antics, frantic foolishness featuring those fabulously frenetic funnymen; continentally celebrated canines; a gracious, graceful garland of lovelies in a flower-filled fantasy from the circus---Garden in the Sky.

"Aristocrats of the animal kingdom, wondrous whirlwinds on wheels; a crazy company of celebrated clowns and peerless practitioners of airborne acrobatics in a dizzying display of graceful grueling gyrations."

Then comes what the program calls "Show Me the Way to Go Home: Danger daringly disregarded by Europe's clown prince of the stratospheric sway-pole," and "the fantastic futuristic fantasy called 'Twas the Night Before Tomorrow."

Now it is intermission time and there's much, much more to come, so fill up with pop corn and peanuts, lemonade and soda pop, and settle back to see and enjoy another full hour of exciting entertainment.

First there is "Beguiling Beauty's Breathtaking Balance," described as "an intrepid, intriguing interlude of trapeze thrills," and "ferocious felines meet their match: A carnivorous cageful of deadly, dangerous denizens of the darkest jungles."

"See it to believe it," says the next title, and the attraction is described as "hereditary hate between tiger and elephant courageously conquered and controlled in a dazzling display of mammal mastery."

There are "Swedish sensations on the silver strand," and "barons and baronesses of baited-breath balancing," then "revelry rules the rings in a nostalgic nod to yesterday," climaxed by "fireman, fireman, save my child!"

"Elegant exponents of equestrian expertise" come next and then "chimp champs create chaos." Watch the "astoundingly agile aerial artisans," then take "a jubilant jungle journey underscored by the reverberating rhythms of Darkest Africa," and see the "pachydermic perambulations and teeterboard thrills never before seen—or dreamed of!"

Here come the "Maniacal masters of matchless manipulations," and next the "celebrated congress of clowns," followed by a "dynamic double dose of trapeze virtuosity."

The final number is "Put on a Happy Face" as clowns capture the center ring and the complete company comes calling to present a captivating circus carnival for children of all ages, "Be a Clown."

Most of the acts are new, billed as "First Time in America," as indeed they are. But the old standbys are there, like Merle Evans, completing half a century of trouping with the Ringling Bros. and Barnum & Bailey Circus, the "Big Bertha" of them all, in an astounding display of personal persistence recognized throughout the world.

Although even close friends and circus officials do not know it and won't believe it when they're told, this is to be Merle's last tour with the circus that has been his life since March, 1919, a span unequalled by any other "windjammer" in the business.

When the season ends in Buffalo, New York, in late November, Merle will step down quietly and with no special ceremony to a life of retirement with his peppery wife, Nena, in their Florida home.

Surely this "Toscanini of the Big Top," this "Will Rogers with a Horn" has earned his rest, but once off the road he will be as busy as ever. At seventy-seven years of age Merle Evans is in remarkable good health and described as a physical phenomenon by some of the most skilled and learned physicians in the country.

He is the sort of individual doctors have in mind when they say the human body is the most perfectly balanced organism in the world, capable of operating year after year with a minimum of attention, and no time out.

Merle is an outstanding example of endurance, having performed at full speed night and day in all kinds of weather and under adverse conditions for a long lifetime without any special treatment or repair, and is still going strong.

Just as some men are destined to become farmers, firemen, or financiers; politicians, policemen, or poets, so was this rugged son from the heart of his beloved America ordained to be a noted horn blower and musician, and a great band leader.

Of all the musical instruments tenderly laid in the hands of children by loving and hopeful parents, and cheerfully endured for years thereafter, only rarely does a towering genius emerge from all those hopes and dreams. Merle is a prime example, a legend in his lifetime.

"Merle Evans is 'Mr. Circus Music' around the world," said the 1969 program. "He's led the brass band of the Greatest Show on Earth for more than 30,000 performances, underscoring the music with 'rides' on the world's loudest cornet . . . .For Merle and Nena, every day is Circus Day---and they wouldn't dream of having it any other way."

*Quotations used by special permission of Ringling Bros.-Barnum & Bailey Combined Shows, Inc."

2

Boy with a Horn

At the time Merle Slease Evans was born on December 26, 1894, his father, John L. Evans, was foreman in a coal mine near the town of Columbus, Kansas. The boy was named for a clothing merchant but he never used his middle name or initial, and has always been plain Merle Evans to circus fans and musicians everywhere.

The Evans family which included the mother, Sarah Elizabeth Stoddard Evans, and two children, had come from Paducah, Kentucky, as pioneers, and hoped to homestead in the Oklahoma territory. But money ran low and they stopped in Columbus, a busy farming and manufacturing community a dozen miles north of the border, in the southeastern corner of the Sunflower State.

The older Evans children were Leila and Willard. After Merle came four others---brothers Homer and Fred, and sisters Ruth and Juanita.

"They were one of the most respected families in Columbus, and all hard workers," said Ned Aitchison, a long-time friend. "As Merle grew up, he was always a very busy boy, not a lazy bone in his body."

While the family lived in modest circumstances, there was a piano in the parlor of the rambling wooden house, and Leila played it very well. The other children, except for Merle, showed no inclination for music. Whatever such talents might have gone into their makeup apparently were concentrated in his sturdy frame.

Anyway, Merle was a human turbine from the very beginning and was earning money in a variety of jobs by the time he was six years old, shining shoes and selling the *Star* and *Journal,* morning and afternoon papers from Kansas City, on the streets of his home town.

He had a paper route, too; he sold the *Saturday Evening Post* and a weekly printed in Williamsport, Pennsylvania, called *The Grit,* which everyone said aptly described his spirit.

From the beginning, Merle liked music and was stoked with ambition, not to become a scholar or banker, but determined to make his way in the world through hard work and industriousness.

Soon after he started selling newspapers he became the proud owner of a cornet which he learned to hold and play with his right hand, little finger extended, while dishing up papers and magazines with his left. The cornet was often used to attract attention to the headlines, thus providing audible advertising for his wares.

"I was a great guy to work," Merle recalls in his short, crisp way of speaking. "My folks were poor and lived on the edge of town. We didn't have a lot of luxuries, but we worked and always managed.

"I was no good in school. Oh, how I hated school---every day of it! I was the shyest, most timid guy you ever laid eyes on; couldn't even speak a piece in class. Every time I got up before my schoolmates I was scared to death. My legs turned to jelly and my mouth dried up. My parents would have been better off if they'd put me in the meat grinder and made fertilizer out of me. It's a fact."

Those years after the turn of the century were times of vitality, peace, and understanding in America, when ambitions and opportunities inspired, or necessity forced, men to honest toil without Works Progress Administration or Social Security.

There were dynamic leaders in every field, or so it seemed---business, engineering, architecture, law, medicine, transportation, and the arts. The automobile and airplane were coming into being and, while still in their infancy, improved as they multiplied.

There were noted orators, great sports figures, and talented performers; fine singers, actors, and musicians. There were great band leaders like Patrick Sarsfield Gilmore, John Philip Sousa, Arthur Pryor, Patrick Conway, Edward Franko Goldman, Herbert Lincoln Clarke, Karl L. King, Henry Fillmore, and many, many more.

There was a piano, organ, or at least a phonograph in every parlor, and people were singing "By the Light of the Silvery Moon," "Down by the Old Mill Stream," "When Irish Eyes are Smiling," "Let Me Call You Sweetheart," "Sweet Adeline," "Bill Bailey, Won't You Please Come Home?" "Shine On Harvest Moon," "On Moonlight Bay," and "When We Come to the End of a Perfect Day."

Thousands of cities and towns throughout the country had silver cornet bands. Usually the leader received a modest salary, but musicians often furnished their own instruments, or these were donated, along with uniforms. Players practiced enthusiastically and faithfully for concerts in the park. It was considered an honor and a privilege to play in the band.

Decoration Day, the Fourth of July, and Labor Day were times to celebrate with parades and fireworks. Bands turned out in gaudy red, white, and blue uniforms, often competing with fife and drum corps from neighboring communities.

Merle Evans' home town had a band, several of whose members worked in the cigar factory or overall factory. The eager young Evans would slip away to the second floor of the old stone building that was the city hall and fire station to hear the band practice.

The band was under direction of Professor Kaholski and had the reputation of being one of the best in the Midwest. Members included the Bowers brothers, Bill McGhie, John Nicholson, Gar Richardson, Harry Hicks, Harry C. Strong, Turkey Thomas, Guy Mitchell, and many others of varying age, including the two Reid brothers who later were to die in a circus train wreck.

The band traveled to other parts of the country and had a standing invitation to the Priest of the Palace parade in Kansas City.

Each Saturday night during the summer the old band wagon would be drawn to each corner of the town square for a two-hour concert. Merle was always on hand to listen and learn. When Bill Bowers became town band director, Columbus decided to organize a children's band. Merle Evans was the first to join.

"I was about ten years old at the time," he remembers. "I guess about twenty of us showed up at this meeting to organize the kids band. I was the first in line. They asked me what instrument I wanted and I says, 'Gimme an alto,' which is something like a French horn. We always called 'em rain catchers because they'd catch the train.

"When the band instruments came, my father hitched the horse to the buggy and went into town to get this horn they'd ordered for me. We lived about a mile or a mile and a half outside of Columbus. But they'd missed sending the alto; sent an extra cornit instead. So my father brought this cornit home and I played it."

The dictionary gives the pronounciation as "kor-net" or "kor-nit" and Merle uses the latter which, with his quick, crisp phonetic translation of the word comes out in a short but pleasing sound of one syllable--"cornit." Many professionals pronounce it "kor-nit" and "klar-nit," just as most circus fold say "kal-ee-op" while the general public calls it "ka-lie-o-pe."

The John Slater cornet his father brought home that day cost $16.95 and was Merle's proudest possession. He never tired of it and carried it with him everywhere. Boyhood chums soon gave him the nickname of "Doc," because he always had his cornet case by his side.

He practiced morning, noon, and night, so long and loud that he almost drove the neighbors out of their minds. His father, responding to their pleas, would make him go to the woodshed and shut the door, but Merle kept blowing.

School officials told him he must not blow the horn in the building. Finally, he was told not to bring it to school or even play within hearing distance of the classrooms. No wonder he lost all interest in scholastic pursuits, and preferred his cornet.

He had an instruction book written by George Southwell and remembers the first number in it was entitled "Our Leader." This was a simple little thing and he quickly learned to play it, with one hand! He bought himself a music stand and took lessons from Bill Bowers, the band leader, with money he'd earned.

"I practiced every chance I got," Merle recalls. "Oh, did I practice! I played in the woodshed, on the back porch, in my room, in the fields, the woods---anywhere I could find the time.

His first public appearance was at the Methodist Church in Columbus, when his Sunday School teacher, Mrs. W. J. Moore, asked him to play. Instead of being embarrassed, Merle happily led the class of nine children in a little march in and around the church, blowing "Onward Christian Soldiers" on his cornet.

His reputation grew, and soon he was known as the loudest cornet in Cherokee County. The band leader once warned him jokingly, "Blow that thing a little harder, Merle, and you'll straighten 'er out." He tried, but in 66 years of blowing has never accomplished the feat.

The children's band of Columbus put on a program in the town theater and took in enough to buy individual chairs. They proudly wrote their names on each and used them at practice and during concerts. When the band finally broke up, Merle took his chair home and kept it for many years.

No matter how much he liked to play the cornet, there wasn't enough money coming in from selling papers, so he added to his income by shining shoes at Fletch Crowder's barber shop.

He left the bootblack job and went to work washing dishes at the Brooks Hotel. A few days afterward, the second cook quit and Merle was promoted. His chores included peeling potatoes, opening cans and jars of corn and beans, and bringing in dirty dishes from the dining room.

Mrs. Brooks did the cooking. Eight regular roomers also took meals there. One was a dour old man named Mears, who owned a paint store and sold what Merle swears was the reddest paint ever concocted by man. It was known as "Mears' Barn Paint" and spotted the Kansas Countryside like measles on a child's face.

Mears wore a fine set of chin whiskers. One day a mischievous boarder named Charlie Taylor suggested to Merle that he "tickle Old Man Mears under the chin and go like a billy goat." Merle thought this was a corking good idea and he carried it out like a trouper the very next time Mears sat down to dinner.

That got our hero out of the Brooks kitchen and dining room immediately and landed him in the front office, where he would be roused out of bed at six o'clock every morning to get at such duties as mopping, sweeping floors, and wrestling luggage.

In addition to its permanent guests, the Brooks clientele included many traveling men known in those days as "drummers," who arrived by train with enormous sample cases and trunks filled with piece goods, dresses, underwear, shirts, ties, and various other items of clothing and shoes in general demand.

One of Merle's duties was to tidy up display rooms and move those drummers' trunks to their proper locations. It was excellent training for the husky lad who was to spend his next dozen years moving from one city to another all across the country, keeping his belongings in one sturdy red trunk until he moved into a stateroom on the circus train.

The spring after Merle's twelfth birthday, he got a job on a farm near Sherwin, Kansas, operated by a bachelor named Don Gassoway, who took a liking to the ambitious boy with the horn and paid him fifty cents a day, three dollars a week, plus room and board.

Gassoway raised wheat, corn, and livestock. He expected the farm hands to be in the fields at sun-up, take an hour off at noon for lunch and a brief rest, then work until dark.

One day Gassoway asked Merle if he'd ever run a plow. "Sure," the cocky youth replied. Of course, he'd never followed a plow but he knew what one looked like, how it worked, and didn't want to take a chance on losing his job.

Gassoway wasn't too sure, so he helped hitch the horses to the plow and make the first round with Merle, walking the mile down the row and back, then leaving the neophyte plow-boy on his own for the rest of the day.

When time came to harvest the wheat, Merle would hitch the horses to a combine and ride up and down until there was only a small patch left in a corner of the field. Then arming himself with a club, he'd wade in and kill the cottontails huddled there.

"They were young and tender; mighty good eating," he says in happy recollection. "Gassoway also had an old black drake that was causing a lot of trouble among his chickens.

"One day he asked me if I wanted the old drake and I says, 'Sure,

I'll take him.' So I took the drake home and put it in with my mother's chickens. Christ! Did we have a commotion in our hen house? My mother took care of that. She killed the old drake and we had it for Sunday dinner."

Merle's job on the Gassoway farm filled nearly all his daylight hours, so he was happy when rain interrupted field work and he could play his cornet.

"I think windjammers are mostly born as well as made," he says. "My parents thought enough of me to pay $16.95 for that old John Slater cornet, and I never lost the desire to play it.

"When I was working all day in the fields, I used to walk a mile and a half to the railroad station at Sherwin and catch a local to Columbus, eight miles away. I'd rehearse with the Columbus Silver Cornet Band until 11 o'clock, then catch a freight that got me back to Sherwin about 1 o'clock in the morning.

"Then I'd walk across those lonesome prairies to my farmhouse room, go to bed, and sleep until daybreak. These days I doubt if you'll find one kid in a million who'd do that. I had ambition; I wanted to be a musician in the worst way."

3

Showboat Down the Mississippi

When his job at the wheat farm played out, Merle went to work at Black's greenhouse, about a mile from the Evans home. One of his chores there was pulling buds off carnations. He is certain he pinched the buds off a million or more young carnations, by hand. Anyway, he figures it helped strengthen his fingers, part of the training that went into making him one of the nation's leading and most durable musicians.

Another greenhouse crop was head lettuce, which had to be cut and thoroughly washed to get the sand out. Then the land could be spaded and planted again, so that when Merle wasn't playing nursemaid to young carnations he was cutting, washing, and planting lettuce.

But he had other jobs, too, like driving a delivery wagon for Campbell & Bradney's grocery, and driving cows to Montsler's pasture at one dollar a month per cow.

He had been blowing his John Slater cornet for a little over two years when he sold it and bought another, a Boston Three-Star from a cigarmaker named Rice who was leaving town and agreed to part with the instrument for thirty dollars in cash.

"I was still enrolled in school at the time but I thoroughly detested it," Merle remembers. "Oh, how I hated arithmetic, spelling, reading, and all the rest of it! On my way to and from school, I'd stop in Johnny Nicholson's little print shop and help him set type for a church paper called *The Truth*.

"I wanted to stay there all day, so I'd hang around until this Johnny Nicholson would tell me I'd better get going or I'd be late for school. Soon as school let out, I'd hurry back and maybe set type for an hour or two. I just was never any good in school. I hated it---never got past the eighth grade."

In the meantime, Merle joined the town band, along with Cap and Owl Lammons, Cecil Huff, Carl Stuckey, and a few others from the kids band. He organized an orchestra to play for dances and signed up as a member of the American Federation of Musicians, local 119. He has been a union musician ever since and also is a member of the very select American Bandmasters' Association.

His real entry in the world of entertainment began the day the powder works blew up in Stippville. This was a community about two miles from Columbus whose industries included a plant of the Atlas Powder Works and a few coal mines.

"Every so often, I think about every three or four years, the powder works would blow up," Merle recalls. "This time when I heard about it, I got a ride over to Stippville on a farm wagon; made the trip on a Saturday just out of curiosity.

"Every year Columbus put on the Old Settlers' Reunion and hundreds of people would come to town; some camped in the city park all week for this big reunion. And we'd always have a carnival play Columbus during this week.

"Coming back from Stippville late that Saturday afternoon I could hear a band blaring out music on the carnival grounds, down by the railroad tracks, so I got down off the wagon and hurried over to see what was going on. If it was music, I wanted to be there. It attracted me like honey draws a fly.

"The S. W. Brundage Carnival Company had set up and it had a seven-piece band led by a fellow named Cleve Pullen. This Pullen was a fabulous character. He had a lot to do with my young life and I'll tell you more about him later.

"Anyway, he played the loudest E-flat clarinet I ever heard; you could hear that squeaky old clarinet ten miles in all directions.

"The Brundage band had a cornet, one trombone, one bass, one baritone, and two drummers. But the cornet spot was open at the time. It seems the last man who had it got involved with a female, got her in a family way, and took off for parts unknown.

"So there I was, listening to the band and Cleve Pullen says to me, he says, 'You a musician?' I says, 'Yes, I play cornet.' Right away he asked me if I wanted the job and I says, 'Certainly; how much you going to pay me?'"

Cleve Pullen demanded a demonstration by the tall, tanned youth, so he asked Merle to give him a few notes on his horn.

"I whipped that cornet out of the case and blew so loud it almost knocked him off his feet. You probably could hear it if you were down in Oklahoma. Anyway, I got the job, at ten dollars a week.

"Before that, I had run away from home when I was thirteen years old. I had joined a little outfit called Mohair's Minstrels, but the job only lasted one night. The boss was Charles Van Dyke Mohair and when he heard my parents' tale of woe and found out my age, he fired me on the spot. I'd only gone as far as Baxter Springs, and my parents took me home.

"On this Brundage job, I had to pay room and board out of the ten dollars, play cornet in the band, and set up and take down the merry-go-round. There were some other chores, too, but I was a bear for work and anxious to join the show.

"Brundage was playing one-week stands and I was told to be at the depot at eight forty-five next morning, which was Sunday. I was happy and excited.

"But when I went home and broke the news, my mother and older sister carried on something awful. Oh, how they shed torrents of tears when I told them I was going out with a carnival! You'd a-thought I was about to commit the unpardonable sin.

"I slept very little that night and could hardly wait to get going with the S. W. Brundage outfit. I showed up at the depot long before they were ready to pull out.

"We loaded everything on three box cars. We had the merry-go-round, a ferris wheel, a dog and pony show; had some concessions like

Merle Evans with the S. W. Brundage Carnival in 1909 (back row, fourth from the left)

knock over the milk bottles and ring the high bell. There was a fun house, too---one of those things where you get a good shaking up and there'd be a lot of laughs.

"We had a black top and would show about twenty minutes of movies for ten cents. A lot of people in Kansas will tell you the first movies they ever saw were in Brundage's black top.

"Brundage would put on a free show every night at ten-thirty and Saturdays at eleven. We had a foot juggler named Jerome Abbey, who was excellent. We had a big boa constrictor, too.

"This old boa constrictor was what's known as a 'good feeder,' and we'd charge a dime to see it. Every Saturday night we'd feed it a chicken or some other small animal, and charge a quarter. You'd be surprised how many people would pay a quarter to see 'em feed this big old snake.

"The first stand after Columbus was Fredonia, and that's where I made my first appearance with the Brundage show. This Brundage was a big outfit; at one time they had two railroad shows and carnivals under canvas, Brundage No. 1 and Brundage No. 2.

"I worked all through the season and we closed at Newkirk, Oklahoma. The show was to winter there. I worked hard that first season and put in long hours, but I was used to hard work and I liked trouping. I guess it was in my blood."

Merle had accumulated thirty dollars when the season ended, which was enough to buy some clothes and a train ticket to Salina, Kansas. His father, selling insurance at the time, had written that he would be in Salina at the National Hotel on a certain day.

Merle hadn't eaten when he boarded the train and spent his last ten cents for an apple, from the news butcher. When he walked into the lobby of the National Hotel he carried a Gladstone bag and his cornet but his pockets were empty. So was his stomach.

He inquired if his father, John L. Evans of Columbus, Kansas was registered there. The answer was no.

Merle walked out, went down the street and heard music in the distance. It was coming from a Salvation Army band. He hurried along, his spirits buoyed by the plaintive tones. Just as he approached the scene, the music stopped.

The little group paused for a brief prayer and announcement, then walked off down the block and around the corner. Merle hurried after it.

When he caught up he approached the leader and whispered that he had no money, no place to sleep, and was a musician out of work. "I play cornet," he said.

The leader, a big man in blue uniform with cap embellished in gold, whirled to grasp his hand in friendly greeting and solemnly intoned, "God bless you, brother! Give us music and we'll give you bread."

The Salvation Army provided Merle with a uniform, gave him food and a place to sleep. In exchange, he gave the volume and tone of his cornet to the music of a mandolin, tambourine, banjo and snare drum. He remembers that Thanksgiving dinner with turkey and all the trimmings was one of the best he ever had.

"I still hadn't finished school but I didn't want to go back, so I decided to get a job," Merle says. "I read an advertisement in the local paper for a man to drive a milk wagon. I applied and got the job."

And so the young cornet player quietly de-frocked himself in favor of steady employment, placing bottles of fresh milk on doorsteps.

He reported to the Salina Sanitary Milk Company at 4 o'clock every morning, but having been an early riser all his life, the pre-dawn hour proved no particular hardship. He would feed the two horses and load the wagon with milk while they ate the hay, then make his first deliveries. Returning to the plant, he would put in another load and take it to another part of town.

He finished his delivery chores by noon, which left ample time to practice. Of course, that didn't satisfy the eager musician. He would take his cornet along on his rounds, to the consternation of late sleepers all over Salina.

The horses knew the route as well as Merle did, so he soon fell into the habit of taking short cuts across vacant lots and meeting the horses on the next block, tootling a few notes along the way, like a mockingbird at sunrise.

One day while he was depositing milk on a doorstep, something frightened the horses and they lunged off down the street, leaving a trail of broken milk bottles and wrecking the wagon. Merle was fired.

He found work at a pool hall in Salina where he racked balls, swept out the place and ran errands, meanwhile still playing his cornet. He wrote a letter to Brundage and in reply was told he could have a job with the band during the approaching season, at twelve dollars a week.

The show was to start its tour in Newkirk and while the pay wasn't much for a cornet player of proven ability with a season's experience, Brundage had an attractive daughter who was about Merle's age, and that was an added incentive. He happily departed Salina for the Sooner state.

"I found out that everybody on a carnival works and works hard," Merle recalls. "This fellow Brundage was an extraordinary man. He was a sincere, religious fellow and wouldn't tolerate any drinking or gambling among his employees.

"He used to advertise, 'We comply with the pure show laws,' whatever that meant---I never found out. I do know that if a young couple came on the show and asked for jobs he'd want to see their marriage license before he hired them.

"And he wouldn't tolerate cussing. I remember he said to me one time, he says, 'Merle, one of the ways to tell if a man is a gentleman or not is to find out if he cusses.'

"That second year I found out Brundage had actually started what he called 'Sunday divine services' for show people. He would invite a local minister in and I'd lead the music.

"It was a very small outfit with the usual mechanical things like ferris wheel, merry-go-round and concessions, a one-ring circus with acrobats, clowns, ponies and dogs.

"But I will say this: Brundage wasn't a hypocrite. He firmly believed in what he was doing. The second year we played Kansas and the Mid-West, people would invite us to be guests in their homes. That's how much they thought of S. W. Brundage.

"As I said, it was a small outfit but I thought it was wonderful. I wasn't disillusioned at all. Every day there was a new experience, new challenge; something to gratify a boy's appetite for adventure.

"I soon got over my homesickness, if I ever had any, but I don't recall that I did. If you once get the smell of sawdust in your system, you'll never get over it.

"Besides, I made friends and met some musicians who knew more than I did, and it was nice to feel I was learning something that would help me get ahead. One of the fellows I met on the Brundage show was Glenn Brunk, one of seven Brunk brothers. At one time later on they had three dramatic shows under canvas.

"Late in 1910 I left the Brundage show and the reason I left was I got a telegram from my old friend Cleve Pullen. He asked me if I'd come with him on the *Cotton Blossom* showboat. I said, 'Certainly.'

"Now this fellow Cleve Pullen was clever. He was an E-flat clarinetist and was a handsome man; could sing and act, too. His partner was Horace Murphy, his brother-in-law, an actor and producer. Pullen and Murphy were married to the Gibbs sisters, Myrtle and Mattie. Murphy was Patrick Gilmore's nephew.

"This *Cotton Blossom* was like most other showboats of the time; never went under its own power but had to be pushed or towed. They were theaters built on barges—actually two or three stories. They were big, brightly painted, sometimes smoky and noisy, but they brought a lot of romance and entertainment to a lot of people.

"The *Cotton Blossom* was a theater with a balcony built all around. It seated about eight or nine hundred and was pushed by a steamer. Four married couples in the company slept on the barge and all single members of the cast, plus the crew, slept on the steamer.

Merle Evans with the S. W. Brundage Shows (second row, behind drum)

"We started out from Paducah and went down the Mississippi; didn't stop at Memphis but played a lot of stands on the way to Baton Rouge. Some were fair-sized towns and some had nothing but river landings---maybe a few stores, or perhaps a town on the rise back of the swamps.

"We had a steam calliope connected to the boiler on the steamer, and every time we'd approach a landing the calliope player would go to work, playing popular numbers.

"The calliope is a chorus of steam whistles---we used to call 'em steam pianos and that's about what they were. They're designed to be heard for miles---nearest thing to sound amplification we had in those days.

"It took a lot of steam to play but you could hear the calliope for miles through those river bottoms. The people would listen and say to the neighbors, 'well, the steamboat's comin'. Then they'd head for the landing.

"It was a free and easy life and I loved every bit of it. I can still smell the sweet, cool air of the mornings and hear the old slap, slap of the Mississippi against the sides of the *Cotton Blossom*.

"I learned a lot and had so much time on my hands I could practice five or six hours a day, which I did, and catch those Mississippi River catfish. I could practice without interruptions on the old *Cotton Blossom*.

"When the boat tied up, we'd pile onto a couple of farm wagons and ride out over the countryside---the band, that is. We had a sixteen-piece band and a cast of ten for the stage show.

"We'd rent those farm wagons and maybe ride four or five miles, blasting away in a sort of parade to let the people know the showboat was in, and we had a good band. People loved band music in those days.

"Then about sunset the calliope would give a thirty-minute concert. That would stir everybody up for miles around. Then the band would take over, playing on the top deck. This would remind everybody the show was about to start. People would come walking through the swamps carrying lanterns, swarming in like a lot of lightning bugs, coming to the *Cotton Blossom*. Oh, those were happy times!

"We'd give part vaudeville and part dramatic shows, like 'The Man and the Maid,' 'The Parish Priest' and other masterpieces of the time. The 'artists' were paid ten dollars a week and 'all,' which meant board and a place to sleep.

"A funny thing happened just before we ended the tour at Baton Rouge. The steamer was in charge of a fellow named Price, we called him 'Captain Price.' He was a little banty-rooster type of a man, wore baggy old trousers and a sea captain's cap he must have had for years and years.

"One day a storm came up and most of us got pretty uneasy. We could see this awful black cloud coming, with thunder and lightning, but the captain told everybody not to worry, said he'd handle the situation.

"He was fairly calm at first but the clouds kept coming, heavy thunder and high wind. So he began to get excited, too, along with the rest of us. By now the wind was churning up big waves, shaking the trees and pushing the boat toward mid-stream.

"Some of the people on board started to panic. This Captain Price, well, he started to holler and yell. He says, 'Throw the anchor over!' I say 'Throw the anchor. Throw the anchor!'

"The deckhands just stood there looking at him and at the clouds. He turned red as a rooster comb and he screams at 'em, 'I told you throw the anchor over!'

"One of the deckhands, a big, burly fellow, stood there with a silly grin on his face and finally he says, 'Cap, there's no line on it.'

"'I don't give a damn about the line,' Price bellows. 'Throw the anchor over!'

"So over the side goes our three hundred and fifty dollar anchor, right in the middle of the Mississippi River."

4

Gabriel Blows his Horn

When the *Cotton Blossom* ended its tour in Baton Rouge, Merle and a few others in the troupe went out as the National Stock Company, giving dramatic shows in small towns.

The climactic feature was a skit called "The Signal of Liberty," and Merle remembers that best for an hilarious ending one night in a community by the bayou. He was the unwilling star.

The tent had been pitched right beside the water and, using a model of the famous battleship Maine, five or six feet long, set in a cradle on the stage, actors would put matches to paper to make smoke and flames, then set off a charge of gunpowder to signal the blowup.

"I was supposed to blow a bugle call," Merle says. "Well, when they get the fire going there was all this excitement---it looked for a minute like things would get out of hand and destroy everything.

"One fellow was scratching a patriotic number on an old fiddle and all hell broke loose. In the confusion, I forget which side the bayou is on and step right off the wharf. I had a rough time trying to blow the bugle call in water up to my neck!

"Anyway, the National Stock Company ended the tour in Lake Charles, Louisiana, and we sent tents, seats, and scenery to Anna, Illinois, for storage.

"Cleve Pullen and I took an eight-piece band and joined the Nigro and Loos Carnival, but it didn't last out the season. So this Cleve Pullen and I formed what we called the Clifton Comedy Company.

"Cleve Pullen was a very voluble and capable fellow who'd been my friend since the Brundage show. He was my best friend, so we went out with what we called a comedy company.

"This was a medicine show with a cast of four. We had Pullen's wife and Billy Dale, an organist and comedian. I played cornet and Pullen

With National Stock Company band in 1910 (third from left, standing)

was the fast-talking promoter and clarinet player. So overnight Cleve becomes 'Doc Pullen.' "

Merle, who is an honest and industrious man, apologizes for this period of his life and the ehtics involved but it was a living and it kept him in show business.

"Now, a boy of fifteen or sixteen is not likely to pay much attention to ethics," Merle explains. "When he is on his own, his chief concern is to get a job---at least mine was. Perhaps that's why I helped run this old-time medicine show.

"Anyhow, we got some film and a motion picture machine, and for fifty dollars we laid in a supply of medicine from a Chicago house. This outfit dealt with medicine shows and they furnished us posters, pills, and liquid to sell as medicine.

"We had thousands of little round pasteboard boxes for the pills; we had vials for the medicine and Doc Pullen to peddle it. We had movies and a three-piece band of cornet, clarinet, and organ. And we had a pretty young dancer, Mrs. Cleve Pullen. We were in business.

"Our first stop was Nashville, Arkansas. We found a vacant store we could rent cheap, fixed up a sort of stage, rounded up some saw-horses and nail kegs, got some boards from a lumber company, and fixed seats for about seventy or eighty people.

"For a dollar and a half we hired a horse and carriage. We wanted to do a little advertising, you see? Cleve would sit up front and Billy Dale was in back with me. We had banners on both sides and any place we'd see people we'd yell, 'Big show tonight; free movies and entertainment. Everything free. Come one, come all! '

"We'd start our show with movies and I'd be back stage packing pills and filling bottles. We could tell by the turnout how much we'd sell. Cleve would come on in claw-hammer coat and looking like a real specialist. When he was dressed in cutaway, with pince-nez and a long black ribbon, he looked very impressive. And his line of patter would make anyone want to buy.

"Billy Dale would play some soft organ music. Cleve had a high opinion of music for drawing people and making 'em buy. He used to say, 'Give a man good music and he'll reach for his pocketbook a whole lot easier.'

"Cleve claimed our medicine was good for anything from falling hair to ground itch. We'd sell these pills for fifteen cents. Cleve's wife would do a serpentine dance.

"Doc Pullen would say this 'Skunk Oil Liniment' was good for man or beast; guaranteed to cure any human ill. He claimed it was especially good for improving the hearing---keep wax out of the ears. Oh, he worked all the angles.

"I'd run a few slides while Cleve changed costume. Then, with Billy Dale at the organ, Cleve would come out and sing, 'In the Shade of the Old Apple Tree.' The song had just come out and it went over big. This Cleve had a good voice, an excellent voice.

"We'd end the show by offering both the pills and skunk oil for a quarter. So, even with free admission, we could take in quite a bit, depending on how many ailments Doc Pullen convinced the people they had.

"The pills came in big jars like pickle jars and we had a barrel of 'Skunk Oil liniment.' It smelled terrible but probably wasn't anything that would hurt you---maybe some glycerin, coloring, and Lake Michigan water.

"Once after listening to Doc Pullen's spiel, I took a big slug of it myself. Whoo-ee! It nearly killed me. None of us knew what was in the medicine or the pills but people would come back for more.

"Nowhere but in Arkansas could we get by with our medicine show. Nowadays, you wouldn't dare sell the stuff anywhere in the United States. They'd throw you in jail and tie the key to a fox's tail."

After working Arkansas, Cleve and Merle went to Wichita for a brief engagement at the Yale Theater. Then they joined Horace Murphy in a show called "Murphy's Comedians," at Sikeston, Missouri.

With Murphy's Comedians' band in 1911 (front row, third from left, cornet tucked under his arm)

In addition to these three, the cast included Joe Baird, Fred Wilson, Charles J. Gary, Nicolas Brunner, Gordon D. Hays, Harry Hays, Harry Laton, Frank Kassel, Fred Curtis, Otto Weikoff, the Gibbs sisters, Mattie and Myrtle; Trixie Franklin, Ruby Kisman, and a tot named Miss Edmond Murphy.

They toured Missouri, Illinois, Arkansas, Mississippi, and Louisiana that summer and fall, giving dramatic performances and peddling a book of songs, with pictures of the entire cast on the cover, for ten cents.

Admission was ten cents and reserved seats cost another dime. Merle was paid seventeen dollars a week but when business dropped off in the fall this was cut to fifteen. Still, it was better than the medicine show, where the ethics never did sit well with him.

Murphy's Comedians ended the tour at Alexandria, Louisiana. This proved a lucky break for Cleve Pullen, singer, orator, supersalesman, and pharmaceutical mountebank, for there he met a bakery owner who had a severe case of show business fever.

The result was Armetta and Pullen's Comedians, with the bakery man a heavy investor. Merle went along as band leader and cornetist, but the show lasted only a few weeks.

So Merle wound up leading the band on the S. W. Brundage Carnival,

On tour with Armetta & Pullen Comedians in 1912, shown here at Roodhouse, Ill., (second from left, seated)

again. By now the show had mushroomed from a three-car outfit to twenty cars. It closed the 1913 season in Bartlesville, Oklahoma. Brundage had an agent named W. M. McQuigg who attempted to organize a show of his own. Plans called for a ten-piece band with Merle as leader. The opening was scheduled for Ottawa, Kansas, but it never came off; no money.

Merle had been on the road with one show or another for about three years now and was out of a job. He went home to Columbus to plan his next move, certain that something would turn up.

He spent a good deal of time chatting with old cronies at Fletch Crowder's barber shop but let it be known he was available as a musician, preferably leading a band.

Within a week a telephone call came offering him a job with Bell, Orndorff and Ballard of Pittsburg, Kansas, promoters of a road show called "Uncle Josh Spruceby's Melodrama." Merle was to play cornet and lead the band, for seventeen dollars a week.

"I always say I joined the Spruceby show in California," he laughs. "The promoters told me I could join up in California---turned out to be California, Missouri!

"We had eleven musicians in the band and I was one of two cornetists as well as leader. We had Rube costumes and everybody doubled. By arrangement, we'd go to different parts of town and play like clowns. Later we'd all meet at one place we'd agreed on, like the courthouse steps or the post office.

"I made up with flowing whiskers and a linen duster, and carried a grip with 'High C Oil' written on the sides. We'd meet and maybe do a concert or parade around the courthouse square. It was a wonderful way to draw a crowd.

"The climax of the program was the saw mill skit. In this the heroine was being pursued by a relentless villain. He was going to get her out of the way so he could come into a fortune, you see? He'd catch her and lash her to a plank in a saw mill.

"There was a real circular blade tearing through two concealed lasts, raising clouds of sawdust and making an ungodly racket. All the while the fair maiden was approaching her doom the orchestra would play what they called 'hurries'---storm music and battle scenes. Oh, it was exciting to the audience, like the climax of a cowboys and Indians movie.

"Well, I was the guy who turned the saw. I sat behind a curtain on a sort of bicycle contrivance and pumped it to run this saw. We had a safety device to stop the girl an inch short of cutting her in two. It was terrifying all right, to the customers.

"Excitement would build up with the girl screaming like a panther in distress. And sometimes women would faint. Just when the maiden stopped short of the saw, a dashing young lover would come to the rescue.

"During all our performances, the girl wasn't nicked once, but I'd had enough acting for a while, so I quit to take the job of band director at Campbell, Missouri. I got fifty dollars a month plus room and board. Nearly every town had a band in those days."

One of Merle's pupils at Campbell was Carl Bailey, who later became governor of Arkansas. But he remembers the town best for an incident that terminated his tenure as band leader and ended his sojourn in Campbell. It involved the most noisy and unrestrained religious group in town and perhaps in the entire state---The Holy Rollers.

"The Cotton Belt railroad ran through town and about two blocks down from the depot was this creek," Merle remembers. "Just over the bridge was a Holy Roller congregation using a big tent for a meeting place. They were having a revival and it went on and on. Sinners were confessing and crying right and left, every night in the week.

"Well, the people began to complain about all this racket keeping them awake nights. So I guess the Holy Rollers heard about it and decided to wind up the meeting, maybe to keep down any trouble.

Anyway, they spread the word around that at nine o'clock on a certain night, Gabriel would blow his trumpet and the world would end.

"Life as the leader and teacher of a small town band wasn't too exciting to a young fellow like me. In fact, it was commencing to get dull. I'd had a taste of trouping with carnivals and showboats; I liked to travel and liked music, but I felt I wasn't getting anywhere.

"So I decided to get out, but I did it in a big way. I used to hang around Albert Herberhold's barber shop and one day it dawned on me, 'Maybe I'll be Gabriel.' I told the policeman---they only had one in the town---I was certain Gabriel wouldn't make the date so I'd fill in for him.

"He thought it was a hell of an idea but he wanted permission from the mayor. So we went to see the mayor and he agreed. I guess he'd had complaints about the noise. Nobody but the three of us knew of my plans.

A few days before Gabriel was to show up, these Holy Rollers began giving their things away---chickens and hogs and even clothes; getting set to meet their God. A lot of 'em were serious, believed the world was going to end.

"Well, the night came and the place was jammed. They were sort of quiet at first but then they warmed up and started singing and praying, begging forgiveness, making a lot of confessions, and promises. Every now and then they'd stop and listen for Gabriel's horn.

"We'd rigged up a spotlight and were all set for Gabriel to step right into it. On the stroke of nine, this white-robed man walked up the creek bank by the bridge, the spotlight picked me up and I started blowing the loudest bugle call ever heard in the state of Missouri. Then I gave 'em a few smears and a couple of extra loud blasts.

"Well, all hell broke loose. Oh, did they take off in all directions? They were knocking over chairs and running over one another trying to get away from there. You never saw such confusion---down the railroad track, through the bushes, into the creek; everywhere people yelling and screaming, praying, and crying, and all of 'em running as fast as they could, scrambling.

"I left town. And to this day I've never been back to Campbell."

5

Life on the 101 Ranch

Merle went back to the S. W. Brundage show, which in 1915 sent out two carnivals, and led the band on one of these. When the season ended, the versatile and durable cornet player joined what was called a " '49 Camp," forerunner of the taxi and jitney dances.

The '49 dancers were dressed in cowgirl custumes, neat and clean, and worked for fifteen cents a dance, which lasted only two or three minutes while the orchestra whipped through a couple of choruses and a smear.

At one end of the dance floor was a bar where small glasses of Coca Cola or ginger pop sold for fifteen cents. The girls used chits for their drinks and these plus the dances could cost a young buck three or four dollars in an evening---a tidy sum to a country boy.

"I didn't stay with this very long," Merle says. "I began to realize that If I was ever going to do anything in music I'd have to aim for bigger things. I liked fine music and I wanted to hear more of it.

"Sousa was a kind of god to me. I once stayed up all night so I could see him and hear his band in St. Louis. I went to Wichita and sent a letter to the Miller Bros. 101 Ranch at Ponca City, Oklahoma. I wanted to know if they had an opening for an experienced band leader and cornet player."

This is a technique Merle has often used. He believes it wise to start at the top, if possible. Usually he reasoned that if there wasn't a band leader's job open at the moment, he'd be available when the time came. And he knew cornet players were more plentiful than band leaders.

"This was my first big chance." he says. "I got the job and was told to organize an eighteen-piece band, for a hundred and eighty dollars a week. That figured to ten dollars a man. So I paid some of my best men twelve or fourteen dollars and others less.

"The Miller Bros 101 Wild West Show's principal attraction was old

Buffalo Bill. No man ever sat in a saddle with more poise than he did. He was a dignified old gentleman, and when he rode in and swept off his hat before an audience, it was something to see.

"When our tour opened at Ponca City, the United States had just finished an engagement with a fellow known as Pancho Villa, down Mexico way. So my band dressed in khaki uniforms.

"We had what I think was the greatest collection of Wild West performers in the country at that time. We had Chester Byers, Tommy Kern; we had the Perry sisters and Johnny Baker, who was Colonel William F. Cody's foster son.

"Baker did a shooting act and so did Buffalo Bill. Even in his old age---he died, I think, at 71---he was a remarkable shot. It was almost automatic with him and he rarely missed a flying target.

"He was a very likeable old gentleman, very fond of music and he'd often stop me at the door of his tent to talk music. He was near the end of his career then and drinking a lot. Oh, did he get loaded!

"The show carried a hundred Indians---a hundred men, women and children. They all slept in one railroad car, in three-decker bunks. Every morning they'd get up early and unload their forty or fifty ponies from another car and ride all over the place. This would stir up dust and create a lot of confusion on and around the show. They also sold moccasins, beads, belts, dolls, and such things.

"The 101 Ranch had what it called a maze. We would bring on a band of Cherokee Indians, a band of Creeks, band of Sioux, maybe a band of Paiutes or Choctaws.

With the Buffalo Bill–101 Ranch Wild West Show in 1916, as band leader and cornetist (second row, extreme right)

"Then there'd be a band of Cossacks from Russia, cowboys from Oklahoma, cowboys from Texas, cowboys from Arizona, New Mexico, Colorado---Christ, the place would be jammed with a hundred and seventy-five, maybe two hundred people.

"Then they'd bring on old Buffalo Bill. He'd ride in and take off his hat and say, 'ladeez an' gentlemen: I take great pleasure in introducing to you my Congress of Rough Riders of the World.'

"The old man was still a superb marksman and after he knocked over a few targets with pistol and rifle they'd put on what we called 'Threading the needle.' These were just a lot of intricate drills, on horseback.

"Then we'd wind up the Wild West show by 'Hanging the Horse Thief.' This was really a thriller. These two or three horsemen would ride in and lie down beside their horses, like they were ready for the night, and pretend sleep. Then the old thief would sneak in and steal one of the horses.

"The cowboys would jump up just in time. They'd start shooting and chasing the thief. They'd tie him up, then drag him around the arena behind their horses.

"This horse thief wore a heavy leather thing, a sort of harness, under his clothes. Oh, he never was hurt but the crowd was certain he'd never live through the shooting and hanging. His biggest gripe was being dragged through the mud or dust.

"At one stand, I remember, we had to cancel the opening. It rained so hard you could hardly see, like a flood. We finally put on a show, for only 28 customers. This was my smallest audience.

"I played for Buffalo Bill's last show. We closed in Portsmouth, Virginia, in that 1916 season and that was his last stand. He's buried on top of Lookout Mountain, near Golden, Colorado. One of the first things you see in the museum there is a picture of me and my 101 Ranch band."

Merle, out of work once more, joined the S. W. Brundage Show for a few days, operating a ball-throwing concession and doing odd jobs until the tour ended in Austin, Texas. Then he teamed with Seth and Eunice Howell on what they called the Archie Clark Carnival, which played only Cotulla, Laredo and Corpus Christi.

There an operator who had a ferris wheel and a merry-go-round became a partner. They rigged up a contraption called a "Spidera Show." This was fitted with mirrors, showed the head and face of a girl and looked like a giant spider.

Each night at nine o'clock the merry-go-round, ferris wheel, and other concessions would shut down while Merle and his musicians went into action with ballyhoo for the '49 show. Things picked up then, especially among the young men.

This was where the money came in, so Merle and the Howells parted company with the Archie Clark group and concentrated on a '49 camp. Seth went ahead to line up stands and Merle organized a band of six pieces.

Their first stop was Robstown, Texas, where they opened as the International Amusement Company, with less than a score in personnel. Biggest headache from the start was finding and keeping dancing girls.

Recruiting efforts met strong resistance from distrusting parents in spite of promises from Eunice Howell to properly chaperone the girls at all times. Mothers and fathers sometimes relented, then changed their minds and came on the show armed with shotguns or six shooters to claim their daughters.

The girls dressed in white middy blouses and blue skirts, their hair tied at the nape of the neck in pigtail style. In such dress they seemed demure but had to act sexy to draw the males.

Applicants were screened somewhat but the company couldn't always be sure of the morals. When one girl was found in bed with a man at a hotel where they were stopping for the night, the show pulled out to protect its reputation, missed the stand, and left the girl behind.

Replacements were always needed. Merle remembers the time he and Seth hired two girls during a church service. A taxi driver told them where one of the girls, who'd just arrived home from a '49 camp, lived and drove them there. At the moment both girls were attending church a few blocks away, so they drove to the church.

The usher invited them in and was disappointed to learn they had not come to worship but insisted on speaking to the two young ladies, who were hired on the spot.

In the town of Liberty City, two young men made an offer to buy the operation, offering to pay fifteen hundred dollars cash and throw in an old Chevrolet touring car. Merle and Seth agreed to sell, and stay on a couple of days to help the new owners get a good start. Things went so well that first night in Llano, the new proprietors refused to obey the 11 o'clock curfew and kept the show open until midnight.

"We warned them they were looking for trouble," Merle recalls. "Townspeople were sure to complain and this would bring heat from the law, but these young fellows said, 'There won't be any trouble.' Next day the law moved in and ordered them to get out of town. They didn't know what to do, but rather than lose the deal we offered a simple solution.

"We said, 'Find out where the city limits end, then get a spot just outside, buy a county license and city authorities can't touch you.'

"They set up and got the license, then decided to do a little advertising downtown. So they paraded the girls in front of the drug store, right down the main street. That was what you'd call rubbing it in.

"Now they were really in trouble. They'd asked for it. Seth and me sized up the situation. We drove around in the old Chevrolet, saw what was going on and decided to get out of there, quick. We started driving and didn't stop until we'd crossed into Oklahoma. Fact is, we drove all the way into Kansas!

"I next toured a while with a little rep show under canvas. I was 'Mr. Brown' in 'The Man and the Maid.' Then I was a race track tout 'In Old Kentucky.' I even played the warden in the prison scene of 'Under Two Flags.'

"But most of my critics said that as an actor I was a pretty good cornet player, so I went back to the 101 Wild West Show. By that time old Buffalo Bill had passed away and Jess Willard was our big attraction.

"The heavyweight champion of the world was no horseman but he would ride into the ring. We'd bring him in with a blare of trumpets and roll of drums. Our announcer, Harry Clarence, would make a spiel about the champion who had defeated Jack Johnson.

Buffalo Bill—101 Ranch Wild West Show band in 1917 (at extreme right)

"Willard would box Walter Monahan, a fellow trouper. One time at Manistree, Michigan, we set up in an open arena and a terrific rainstorm hit about the same time. It rained so hard the boxers couldn't go on. The fans got so mad they made off with eight hundred dollars worth of our folding chairs.

"The show that year was a run-down, grafting outfit and we closed in Jacksonville, Florida. I was glad to get away from it. I got a job playing cornet in Joe Berry's band and rented myself an apartment.

"One day Sylvia Andrews, who had an eighteen-foot boa constrictor and a smaller snake, asked me to help her take the snakes downtown. She carried the small snake and we crammed the big one in a suitcase. I was to be the porter.

"We boarded the streetcar along with some other passengers and along the way picked up more riders. That big boa didn't like his tight quarters and slithered out. He started crawling down the aisle and under the seats.

"Well, the passengers panicked, scattering and emptying the car in nothing flat. We finished the ride with nobody aboard but a nervous and apprehensive motorman, Sylvia and me."

When Gus Hill's Minstrels came to town the job of band leader was open and Merle got it. There were sixty persons on the show, twenty-eight in the band. Merle was happy.

"It was a good band, an excellent band," he says. "Sometimes I wonder if people today realize the popular demand for music in those days. Minstrel shows supplied this need for nearly a hundred years, from before the Civil War to well into the 1920s and 1930s. This country grew up on good entertainment.

"I stayed with the show until we hit St. Louis, then went back with Brundage. I joined it in Austin, Texas, and we closed in St. Joe, Missouri. I had an offer in Omaha, so I went there and signed up ten musicians for the Pearce Carnival. It gave one performance.

"So I joined the Walter Savage Stock Company in Atkinson, Nebraska, This was a busy, money-making outfit, and clean! Why, we made so much money they'd put it in sacks and every night they'd leave these sacks of money lying on the floor, like so much baggage.

"Our twelve-piece band would make three downtown stands to drum up business. The tent seated about fifteen hundred; we had a lot of rides and a lot of other cash grabbers like ball and dart games---even a mitt (fortune teller's) joint. A carnival and stock company. They made so much money I got a bonus! "

6

To the Top of the Mountain

Merle went to Sioux City, Iowa, late in the summer of 1918 to catch the Ringling Bros. Circus. He called on his old friend, Johnny Richards, the band leader, but the reunion could be described as brief and frosty.

They had known each other for years and had grown up in towns only eighteen miles apart but the circus band leader seemed rather cool that day and had little to say.

"I'm still not sure if he thought I was after his job or why he didn't act a little more friendly," Merle remembers. "We only exchanged a few words but I had a talk with Lew Graham, who was in charge of the side show. Lew told me he'd heard there might be an opening for a band leader next season. Nothing definite, of course.

"I was free at the time, so Seth Howell and I went into partnership. We decided to hop-scotch around a little bit."

Seth had a home in Lyons, Nebraska, so they operated out of there. They bought one hundred Victrolas and six hundred popular records from a Chicago company for five hundred dollars.

Seth still had the old Chevrolet and every day they'd load it with Victrolas and records to peddle among rural residents of Iowa and Nebraska. Every time they saw a farmer working in his fields or around the barn they'd approach him like bird dogs on the hunt, Victrola wound up and ready to play.

"We'd sell the Victrola and six records for only seven-fifty. If the farmer wanted his wife and children to hear it, we'd go to his home and play it right there in the parlor. They couldn't turn us down---cash on the barrel head.

"After we'd sold the Victrolas, I got a job playing cornet in a thirty-piece orchestra. We played for a war drama called 'Hearts of the World,' a patriotic sort of thing; very popular in those days. We toured from Kansas City to Salina, where we had to close on account of the flu epidemic.

"So I joined Brunk's Comedians. I'd met Glenn Brunk back in 1910 when I was with the Brundage show. He was one of seven brothers. Oh, they had quite an operation. At one time they had three dramatic shows under canvas.

"I guess I got my first break toward the Ringling show that fall when I was playing cornet with a minstrel show in a theater in Cincinnati. Charlie Wilson, the railroad superintendent for the Ringlings, was there and I had a talk with him.

"We discussed show business and the outlook for next season; with the flu epidemic and the war just over nobody knew what the next year would bring; everything was in a sort of turmoil.

"Anyway, I told Charlie Wilson where he could reach me if anything turned up. I said I'd be working with Brunk's Comedians, out of Wichita."

The Ringlings had a lot of admiration for their trainmaster; even named a town after him, between Ardmore and Ringling, Oklahoma. They listened when Charlie Wilson told Charles Ringling he knew a cornet player named Merle Evans who was a fine musician, experienced band leader, and available.

So it happened that Merle had been playing cornet for fifteen years and was just short of his twenty-fifth birthday when he reached the peak of his mountain in the music world. Word came in a telegram delivered one morning shortly before Christmas of 1918, signed and sent by Charles Ringling, one of five founding brothers of the circus bearing their name. It read:

HAVE POSITION FOR YOU AS LEADER OF RINGLING CIRCUS BAND. REPORT AT YOUR EARLIEST CONVENIENCE.

"Leader of the circus band! " What musician could ask for more? "Report at your earliest convenience! " That would be Charles Edward Ringling, a considerate man who said not a word about salary or even asked if he'd accept. Of course he would!

Ringling's responsibility on the gigantic circus he and his brothers planned was to get the best musicians available for the band, pacify volatile performers and burly workingmen, and oversee the whole operation, usually from the back yard.

At this time the Ringlings, kings of the circus domain in America, had never laid eyes on Merle Evans but they knew his qualifications. They didn't need to mention salary because they knew the job on their new show would be one of the most coveted and prestigious in the country.

"I knew who he was, all right," Merle recalls, "but I'd never met him or any of his brothers. I got the telegram---it was a night letter---at the hotel in Wichita where I was staying. I was leading the orchestra with Brunk's Comedians at the time.

"Was I thrilled? Oh, you bet I was. I thought this would be a wonderful opportunity for me, which it was. I knew they'd be fair with the salary; it had to be more than I was making. And it was a great honor to be band leader on the Ringling show."

Destiny seems to have brought Ringling and Evans together at a most opportune time. The influenza epidemic and war-time transportation problems had plagued all circuses throughout the 1918 season and forced many of them to give up.

The two biggest made the best of it as long as they could, fighting scarcities and curtailed travel, selling Liberty Bonds at every stand and trying to keep morale up on the home front, but they had to cut short the season.

The Ringling show closed at Waycross, Georgia, on October 8th while Barnum & Bailey ended the tour at Houston, Texas, the same day. Both headed for Bridgeport, Connecticut, confirming rumors that the Ringlings were pulling out of their home town of Baraboo after many threats to do so.

The Barnum & Bailey show had maintained winter quarters at Bridgeport since Phineas T. Barnum's day but it wasn't swallowing the Ringling show; rather it was to be a happy marriage of the two.

The vast circus properties were trimmed to fit into ninety-two railroad cars amid many rumors of which acts and attractions might be aboard. It was a time of great uncertainty and nobody from the highest executive to the humblest workingman knew what lay ahead.

Merle stayed with Brunk's Comedians through the winter and spent a few days with relatives in Columbus before heading east to take the circus band director's job. The Ringlings had two capable band leaders but had decided to get rid of them and hire Evans for the new job.

Karl L. King had been director on the Barnum & Bailey show but he didn't stand in too well with the owners because he'd only recently been married and would take off on trips with his bride, leaving the job to his assistant.

John Ringling found out about it and didn't like it at all. He insisted that every man on his payroll work and produce. King made up his mind he didn't want the job on the new show, and the feeling was mutual.

John J. Richards wielded the baton on the Ringling Circus but the owners decided he was playing too much concert music and not enough

RINGLING BROS.

Sarasota Fla Jan 18 1919

Mr Merle Evans;
Wichita,Kas.
Dear Sir;

In accordance with correspondence we are enclosing contracts for season of 1919 as band Director. Please sign and return a copy and reatin the other. We presume that you are familiar in every way with the requirements but mention briefly those that may need explanation now. You understand ofcourse that you are to engage the men. We will send you a lot of blank contracts in a dya or so
Number of men --- thirty-two including yourself
Approximate average of salary for men-- $19.00 per week
That is what we averaged in 1918 and was a little more than in previous years. The lowest was $14--and the highest $24.00 per man.
Approximate date for rehearsal in New York City--March 24th.
We pay a weekly allowance for board during rehearsals and also during the New York engagement--Salaries begin at first performance.
Our preference is to keep the "brass" strong not to weaken it in favor of "Reed" section. We regard the music for the circus performance and the street parade as first to be considered rather than organizing primarily for the "Concert" program preceeding the show.
For Street Parade the Band of 32 should be divided as follows;
First Band Wagon--16 mouth-pieces and your two drummers--18 men
Mounted Band----- 12 Mouth-pieces-show to furnish players
                  cymbals and two drums.-----------------12 men
Usher's Band.You to supply two men-prefer cor & Tromb or
                  Clarionet and tromb------------------- 2 men
                                                         32 men

For inside work--we want a first class piano player to play the Air calliope--if you have one in mind or can engage one advise me.
We use brass (no string) for our after show(suggest 2 cor--2 clari-- 2 horns--tromb--Bass and drums) These men may be excused from playing the Hippodrome races. Please advise me if you understand everything. You may return the signed contract to Sarasota Fla

Yours truly

Letter of instructions from Ringling to his new band leader whom he had never seen circusy stuff. This was in contrast with their feelings in earlier years when they provided patrons with a free band concert for a full hour prior to each performance.

In a letter written by Charles Ringling from Sarasota, Florida, to Merle Evans in Wichita on January 18, 1919, the circus man gave his new band leader specific instructions.

He was to hire thirty-one musicians at an average salary of nineteen dollars a week, based on the 1918 pay scale which ranged from fourteen to twenty-four dollars per man. Merle had used this arrangement himself many times, allowing more for key players than some others. His salary was to be sixty dollars a week.

A list of musicians in both circus bands was sent to him, with the word he was free to hire any of these or any others he wished; his assignment was to get the very best available.

Rehearsals were to begin in Madison Square Garden in New York on March 24 and the show was to open five days later. Musicians were to be allowed five dollars a day during rehearsals and for the New York engagement, to pay for food and lodging. Their pay was to start with the first performance.

"Our preference is to keep the brass strong, not to weaken it in favor of the reed section," Charles wrote. "We regard the music for the circus performance and the street parade as first to be considered rather than organizing primarily for the concert program preceding the show."

For the street parade, he said, the band was to have sixteen mouthpieces and two drummers on the first band wagon, and a mounted band of twelve mouthpieces, plus two men in the usher's band, preferably cornet and trombone.

Charles also said he wanted "A first class piano player for the air calliope," and wrote that if Merle had one in mind, "advise us." He noted "We use brass for our after show" and recommended that this include two cornets, two clarinets and two trombones, plus bass and drums.

Thus Merle began hiring musicians for his first Ringling Bros. and Barnum & Bailey Combined Circus band, keeping in mind that they would need to play more than two hundred cues or portions of numbers during each performance and must be geared for quick and unexpected changes.

First, he would get a rough sketch of the program from the director, then an idea of how the show would be staged from the choreographer. He must consider the tempo of every act, select the music certain performers preferred and blend it all into a pleasing presentation for the show which was to run a strict two hours and twenty minutes.

In addition, he must be prepared to deal with every type of personality, people of all colors and creeds from all parts of the world, and satisfy their musical appetites.

He would need the talent of a Toscanini, the wit and philosophy of a Will Rogers, and the wind power and durability of a legendary Gabriel. He had an abundance of each.

When he reached New York, he had brought along Paul Davis, an experienced alto player from Brunk's Comedians who was to stay with him for thirty-two years. Davis also played with Sousa's and Arthur Pryor's bands, and the Atlanta and Houston Symphony orchestras.

"Al Baker sent me a list of the 101 Wild West Show band," Merle reports. "I'd been with them and they knew what to do; what type of music I wanted. I got two musicians from Kentucky and one from Michigan.

"I brought in ten from the 101 Wild West band and hired some from the old Ringling and Barnum & Bailey bands. My main band would ride in the enormous Two Hemispheres band wagon and there'd be a mounted band in the parade. Oh, we had plenty of music.

"I had thirty-six musicians and five days to get ready for the performance and blend their music into a circus band worthy of the Ringling name; the Ringlings were noted for good music on their shows.

"I looked like a real rube when I first hit New York in the middle of March, 1919. I'd played all over the country but had never made the Big Town. I had on high top shoes and I wore a checkered cap. I had my belongings in a Gladstone bag and I had my cornet.

"This was a Besson cornet I'd picked up in Alexandria, Louisiana. A doctor there owned it and when we saw it Horace Murphy says to me, 'Find out if he'll sell it and how much he wants.' The doctor said he paid seventy-five dollars for it but would take fifty.

"I didn't have the money right then, so Horace Murphy bought it for me. I used this horn for twenty-eight years. Then I sent it up to the Circus World Museum in Baraboo and it's still there.

"Anyway, when I first joined the Ringling show I really looked like a rube, a hayseed from Kansas. After I arrived, John Ringling took a look at me one day and he says, 'My God, what have we got here? Put some clothes on this young fellow---dress him up.'

"At that time I'd never been to New York in my life, and never had any fancy clothes. I was a country boy."

He had keen, sparkling blue eyes; teeth so durable he still has the originals, and a good business head. His hearing was perfect, his reflexes good. He stood five feet eleven but he weighed only a hundred and twenty-eight pounds, most of it sinew and muscle.

Merle Evans in his first appearance in 1919 in Madison Square Garden as leader of the band of Ringling Bros. and Barnum & Bailey Circus

He was a handsome, friendly fellow with a ready smile, an abundance of homespun wit, and an even temper. He had come up the hard way, could play the cornet with one hand or both, liked to travel, loved pop corn; was quick-thinking, agile, and durable; healthy as an ox.

This remarkable man had trained himself in music and had played his beloved cornet on carnivals, aboard a showboat, in Wild West shows and even as a member of a Salvation Army band. He'd played for dances, led bands and orchestras and taught a town band.

Surely no other young man of his time had a more complete and varied background in popular music or was better qualified and equipped to lead the band on the great new Ringling Bros. and Barnum & Bailey Combined Shows, admittedly the toughest and most demanding job in the field of music.

7

In The Garden

Some men seem to have been born to fit the moment, or make the most of it. This is true not only of Merle Evans but of many, many more, including the five Ringling brothers from a family of seven sons and a daughter.

They started their little circus in their home town of Baraboo after trouping for two seasons in what was known as a "hall show," first called the "Classic and Comic Concert Co." and later the "Grand Carnival of Fun."

They took a partner to start their circus, an old man named Fayette Lodawick (Yankee) Robinson, who had a considerable reputation as a showman but was down on his luck at the time. They called it the "Yankee Robinson & Ringling Bros. Great Double Show, Circus and Caravan," and gave their first performance in Baraboo on Monday, May 19, 1884.

They had nine wagons, some seats, canvas, and other equipment, a few mangy animals and an abundance of drive and determination, plus some talent as musicians and entertainers.

Working like mules, they expanded to go on rails in 1890 and when James A. Bailey died in 1906 were in position to buy the large and reputable Barnum & Bailey Circus for $410,000.

Operating these two great outdoor amusement enterprises as separate units through the 1918 season, they prospered and poured money into many enterprises from New York to Florida and west to Montana.

Albrecht or Al Ringling built a mansion in his home town, a large affair of brick, stone, and marble with three floors and a basement, which years later was sold to the Baraboo Elks Club and is still in use. He also built a modern theater that is still in operation.

Alf T. established residence at Oak Ridge, New Jersey, where he conducted extensive experiments in plant breeding and animal husbandry. He also was interested in a plan to raise wild animals in the Florida Panhandle to supply the circus' needs, but this project died in the 1920s land boom.

Otto, treasurer of the clan, was the only one who never took a wife and confined his energies to watching the till. In the early days he squirreled away every nickel and dime he could, and when the brothers needed cash, he doled it out.

Otto often argued with the others over finances and would not tolerate waste. He traveled by horse and buggy or street car while the brothers rode in limousines with chauffeurs at the wheel. He hated ostentation, was known on the lot as "The Little King," and was considered a skinflint by those in his employ.

Al and Otto had passed on along the Sawdust Trail and Alf T. was in such poor physical condition he could no longer plan the spectacles or write music for the ballets and tableaux, as he had done for many years, and went to the land of Red Wagons and High Canvas in October, 1919.

Thus the two younger brothers, Charles and John, were largely responsible for combining the two big circuses into one, operating it through those golden years after World War I and making it truly "The Greatest Show on Earth." To Merle's advantage, he knew them well.

Charles, the most human and understanding of the lot, liked to follow his younger brother's lead in making investments. These frequently turned out to his advantage, but the brothers didn't always agree and had some violent arguments. Charles generally capitulated to the wishes of John, whom he called "My big brother."

Charles knew all the performers personally and most of the workingmen among the more than 1,200 in the giant circus family. He spent a good deal of time with the show, either aboard his luxurious railroad car on the train or in a folding chair in the back yard, where he chatted with performers and gave orders and advice in a fraternal atmosphere.

He was the heart of the operation, in command on the lot---if John wasn't present---and known to all as "Mr. Charlie" to distinguish him from the more bombastic John, who was recognized outside the circus family as "Mr. Ringling." '

John was a flamboyant promoter and big operator who personified the circus. Standing well over six feet tall and weighing more than two hundred pounds, he dressed in the height of fashion, even to Homburg hat and gold-headed cane, and liked Havana cigars.

In his early days he was something of a musician, dancer, and clown but when he left the boards he shed his wooden shoes and dancing slippers in favor of footwear made of alligator skin. He routed the shows and knew America as well as any man alive, even to the amount of business the circus could expect in a given city at a given time, names of railroads leading to it and length of sidings.

After their circus went on rails, John spent little time with it, routing and representing their shows but leaving the headaches of operation to his brothers. He would be a hundred or a thousand miles ahead---making deals, proposals, and promises; entertaining or more often being entertained by his well-heeled cronies.

He was a shrewd and crafty man not only in buying supplies for the circus but in bargaining for real estate, ranchlands, railroads, hotels, and beach property. These, along with income from the circus, made him one of the richest men of his time, and he once ranked among the top twenty in the lucre league.

He built a mansion in Florida where he liked to spend part of each winter promoting real estate and entertaining poker-playing friends from New York, Chicago, Cincinnati, and other cities along with politicians from Washington and Jersey City, during the Warren G. Harding administration and the Mayor Frank (Boss) Hague era.

John took a liking to art and especially that of the Renaissance period. He once told friends he had invested more than eleven million dollars in paintings and sculpture, most of it in Italy, France, and England. He built a museum to house it and opened an art school nearby.

Today the John and Mable Ringling Museum of Art, owned and operated by the state of Florida, ranks among the finest in the country. His mansion and the surrounding properties, including the Asolo Theater and the Ringling Museum of the Circus, also are under state supervision.

Charles followed John to Florida and also built a mansion there. He financed construction of a hotel and several business buildings, started a real estate project, and opened a bank. John had an even larger real estate development and also owned a bank.

The mansion Charles built remained with his estate until recent years when it became the nucleus of New College, a well-regarded institution of higher learning.

At the time the two circuses were being combined, John was supervising the work in twice-a-week tours by limousine from his Fifth Avenue apartment to Bridgeport with Fred Bradna or one of the other executives, while Charles was giving advice and making suggestions from his Sarasota home. The turmoil was understandable.

Charles Ringling had sent Merle blanks to fill in measurements for uniforms for himself and the musicians he had hired. These would be tailor-made. They were of bright green, with a lot of brass buttons, while Merle's uniform had gold braid in generous quantities splashed on chest, arms and shoulders.

The jackets were cut military style, form-fitting with collars closed around the neck, which not only forced the men to hold their heads high but allowed no ventilation, thus adding body heat to their discomfort.

"They were gaudy but they were hot, too," Merle recalls. "We had to rehearse in the worst old place you can imagine. It was high up in the loft in Madison Square Garden and you had to climb old narrow stairs to get there. I still don't know how we got our instruments up there.

"But Mr. Ringling found the place all right. He showed up during one of our early rehearsals. He listened and waited around until we took a break, then introduced himself. It was the first time I'd ever met any of the Ringlings. He asked how everything was going and I said 'Fine.' I told him I thought we'd be in good shape for the opening, which we were.

"We opened with a matinee on Saturday afternoon, the 29th of March. The Garden, in those days before air conditioning, was hot but it was packed as usual for the opening. It was the first of three Madison Square Gardens I played in with the circus.

"We had bright new uniforms and every member of the band sat like he was starched. I stood in front, with my cornet. I felt real important, real proud. I'd come a long way, for a country boy from Kansas.

"For the grand entry I'd picked a number called 'Crescent City,' a lively march that gave the woodwinds a good chance to be heard. I'd said to my men, 'Give it all you've got, boys,' and they did. It was excellent.

"When the matinee was over, John Ringling made his way through the crowd. I could see him coming, heading for the bandstand. I wondered what he had in mind.

"'Young man,' he says to me, 'I like the way you handle that horn. When you were in that grand entry, you damned near blew me out of my box.'

"It was one of the nicest compliments I ever had."

8

No Smooth Sailing

But if things were going well with the band, they weren't running so smoothly backstage. In fact, even before the opening, the Ringlings were having problems with the top echelon, and there were more to come.

Johnny Agee, who had been equestrian director on the Ringling Circus, expected to keep the job as stage manager and master of ceremonies when the shows combined.

Fred Bradna had held the same job on the Barnum & Bailey show and had been with it since 1902, along with his wife, Ella, a featured performer. The Bradnas figured they had the inside track.

Charles Ringling had always been friendly toward Agee, considered him capable, his services entirely satisfactory and had promised him the job when the circuses were combined.

But Bradna, a Teutonic type, had been John Ringling's close friend and drinking companion. On the several occasions when Bradna brought up the subject of his future employment, John promised, "I'll take care of you."

This Bradna interpreted to mean he'd have the job of equestrian director and his wife would continue to be featured in the center ring.

John Ringling had the last say, as usual, after a bitter argument with his older brother. He told Charles to tell Agee that Bradna would be the equestrian director.

With that Agee departed for California and Bradna came down with sleeping sickness. Even Bradna's wife thought he wouldn't make it, and signed a contract to protect herself.

The Ringlings were in a real bind, without anybody to direct the show, so they telegraphed Agee and asked him to come back. He agreed, only on condition that he'd have an iron-clad contract guaranteeing him the title of equestrian director and the salary to go with it as long as he wished.

About two weeks after the show opened, Bradna made a remarkable recovery and showed up in the Garden ready to meet and talk with his friend, John Ringling, who was still on the scene. Fred went to the front office where John and Charles Ringling conferred.

"My Big Brother here has an idea," Charles said. "Agee is guaranteed the title of equestrian director as long as he stays with us but there's no reason why a circus this size can't have a 'general equestrian director' too."

That was perfectly all right with Bradna, so long as he had the title, Ella performed in the center ring and they kept their compartment on the train. Agee could be equestrian director but Bradna would out-rank him, in his opinion, with "general" in front of his title.

Agee had trouped with the Ringlings many years and was made equestrian director when Al died in 1916. As a capable showman, he didn't like the arrangement but he stayed through the season. Later he directed the Tom Mix Circus and then trained horses for movie star Gene Autry.

"I'll say that in 1919 we had the greatest array of stars ever seen on any show," Merle enthuses in happy memory. "We had talent everywhere---a lot of it; top performers and acts from both big circuses.

"Lillian Leitzel, who performed on Roman rings and a swiveled rope high above the center ring, was the greatest ever, in my opinion. And I think most circus authorities will agree. I've never seen her equal in all my time."

Miss Leitzel charmed the audience from the moment she stood in the performers' entrance with the house lights dimmed and a spotlight picking out her tiny, glittering figure. She had an unusual body in that it was small from the waist down but her arms and shoulders were like a wrestler's.

With appropriate fanfare from Merle's band and before a hushed crowd, she would move slowly to the center of the vast arena, her footman and maid trailing behind. The way she walked added to the drama and captivated the crowd. Also, the contrast was stunning because she stood only four feet ten while the footman, Willie Mosher, was six feet four and wore the gaudy uniform of a hotel doorman, with a shak-o two feet high.

Mabel Clemens, the maid, brought up the rear and would pause at the edge of the hippodrome track while Mosher followed Miss Leitzel into the ring, where she would pause dramatically, slip out of her ankle-length cape and kick off her slippers.

While Merle and his band played her favorite waltz, "The Crimson Petal," she would grasp the rope, turn and twist her body until she reached the top, then perform like a bird on the wing for six full minutes while the band played "The William Tell Overture."

Then she'd do her specialty, the plange. Using her right arm and shoulder as an axis, she would propel her body over and over while the crowd sat in hushed admiration. Finally, it would chant and count as she continued, faster and faster to "The Flight of the Bumblebee."

Once as a publicity stunt Miss Leitzel completed 243 turns or planges, a most remarkable combination of skill, strength, and endurance.

She had a double stateroom on the train and it contained a piano

Three circus notables of the 1920's, left to right: Dexter Fellows, the noted press agent; Lillian Leitzel, the famous performer, and Fred Worrell, circus manager

which Miss Leitzel played very well. With all her talent, she could go into towering rages and at times wheedle from the management concessions other stars dared not ask, including a luxurious dressing tent.

"She was very temperamental but I got along with her very well," Merle Evans says. "In fact, I went to Europe with her in 1922 when she appeared with the Bertram Mills International Circus in London.

"I scored an arrangement of 'The Dance of the Hours' from the opera 'La Gioconda' to fit her act, which was a sensation on our show every year through the 1930 season."

Miss Leitzel, once married to Clyde Ingalls, the side show manager, later became the wife of Alfredo Codona, the famous flyer. She fell to her death in Copenhagen, Denmark, on February 13, 1931, while on a winter tour.

What made Lillian Leitzel especially popular with the musicians were little things she'd do. For example, when she first heard the music played for her she'd give each of the drummers---snare and bass---twenty dollars. The drums added greatly to her acts and she was appreciative.

A passing note on Willie Mosher is that he also was a clown. He would bring in a donkey, spread his legs, and the animal would walk between them, producing roars of laughter.

Merle remembers other great performers of those vintage years---Bird Millman, the Wirth family, the Valdos, Pallenberg's bears, George Hanneford family, Edna and Denny Curtis, the Davenports, Jung brothers, Charles Siegrist, the Clarkonians and Orrin Davenport.

Bird Millman was a petite and charming artiste who gave a beautiful performance on the tight wire without a balancing umbrella, the first American to perform in this manner.

She danced waltzes, one-steps and did cakewalks while a chorus of eight voices sang popular selections, then a Hawaiian dance while the chorus sang "Aloha." She had personality and charm.

May Wirth, an Australian beauty, started performing as a child and became the only woman to do a forward somersault on a horse. With her back turned to the horse's head, she'd somersault and twist to land facing forward while the steed galloped around the ring.

She duplicated many riding tricks performed by male equestrians and was tremendously popular in the back yard. The band played quadrilles when she performed, then switched to "Jingle Bells" to bring on the clowns.

"They'd all come running in and while they were dashing around the track, whistling and hollering, May Wirth would keep riding," Merle recalls. "Then she'd stop the horse and the clowns would do a few

Typical crowd under the Big Top in the 1920's

tricks—we'd call it 'stalling'—and May would do another routine.

"We'd play another quadrille and then maybe a fast galop. She was a fine performer, marvelous performer. We'll never see another like May Wirth.

"Poodles Hanneford, the great bareback rider and clown, had come from the Barnum & Bailey Circus, along with Charlie Siegrist. Hanneford was a superb horseman and could leap on and off a horse almost as fast as you could count. He performed with the Hanneford family in the center ring for years.

"Siegrist was a remarkable athlete, too. He worked as a horseman, tumbler, leaper, flyer, juggler and clown. He could duplicate just about any act he ever saw in the ring. Double somersaults were play for him.

"Orrin Davenport—did I tell you about him? He was an equestrian acrobat who did backward somersaults from one horse to another, a second somersault to a third and then a backflip to the ground. Davenport also pioneered indoor circuses in this country. He was a great showman.

"The Clarkonians, Ernie and Charles, had a good flying act and Ernie was the first man to do the triple somersault. Ernie once said he and his brother practiced the double somersault and pirouette nine thousand times before exhibiting it in public.

"The triple, Ernie used to say, was similar to the double somersault and pirouette except that a third somersault replaced the pirouette. He said the triple required only about two years rehearsal because a lot of the preliminary work had been done.

"And the clowns! Who could forget those masters of mirth; the fabulous, foolish, funny-faced clowns of the circus' glory days?

"Who were my favorites? Why, all of them. I love the clowns—good ones, that is. I'd say Jules Turnour, Charlie Smith, Pat Valdo, Eddie Nimmo and Spader Johnson were among the best. They were all fine entertainers and crowd pleasers. Some were musicians and acrobats as well as clowns. Emmett Kelly is a good clown, so is Otto Griebling.

"Each of my favorites had his own style makeup, his own specialty. One of Spader Johnson's best stunts was to walk along the hippodrome track and trip himself, turn a forward somersault and open an umbrella. He also was an excellent cornet player and worked in minstrels.

"I still remember that opening in Madison Square Garden in 1919. It was a fine show, an excellent show; beautiful display of living statues, great acts and the climax with chariot races. They discontinued the chariot races several years later, after one struck and killed a policeman in Philadelphia.

"But getting back to that first show in the Garden. Of course, it wasn't all pop corn and candy apples. They'd settled on Agee as equestrian director and he did a good job. But there was more trouble brewing.

"After the opening performance, people from the musicians union collared circus officials with their demands. They said in so many words, 'You've got to pay your musicians more money.'

"Joe Webber represented the union. He told the Ringlings they must pay a minimum of twenty-five dollars per man per week. John Ringling hollered like a stuck pig. Charles was more reasonable and he began to do some figuring. They asked me what I thought.

"I'd been union all my life but I wanted to be fair to both sides. I'd brought these men here and I didn't want a walkout or strike or trouble of any kind. I wanted to keep all the men I had and make up a good band, one worthy of the circus.

"So I says, 'Let's see what we can pay.' But the Ringlings were opposed to paying twenty-five dollars a man. They just wouldn't pay it. So Charles Ringling told me to drop twelve musicians, just like that.

"Well, we dropped a dozen men right off the reel and I wound up with four trombones, two basses, four cornets, four clarinets, a piccolo, two horns---twenty-four men in all. This gave us a pretty good circus band.

"I still have all the names of those in that first band. Only four of them are still living. Here they are:

"Piccolo--Bert Affeld; E-flat clarinet--Martin Hoexter; clarinets--Tony Ramirez, Robin Booth, George Warner, Pete Sturgis; cornets--Charles Beach, Rhee Gibler, George Platt, Henry Harmon.

"Horns--Paul Davis, Andy Wetterman, Al Baker; baritones--Hugo Helander, Bob Dalziel; trombones--J. C. Phail, Kent Kyes, Gene Miller, Ruppert Hubbard; basses--Tom Dobie, Joker Salziel; drummers--Wilbur Weirek, Hank Young; calliope--R. Louis Sanderson; band master--Merle Evans."

Merle was embarrassed and dejected over events of the evening. It grieved him to drop those twelve fine musicians he'd just hired and rehearsed but there was no other way.

The noted band leader is known throughout circusdom for his honesty and square dealing but he also is famous for his frugality and economy. Although the day had brought troubles and disappointment, an hour of pure enjoyment was ahead.

"After the show was over," Merle recalls with his usual enthusiasm, "Agee comes running over to the band, threw his arms around me to thank me and told me how good my band was. Then he took me out to dinner. The food was excellent and we had a wonderful time!"

Music for the Circus

No other musical group in the world is quite like a circus band. It has coordination, rhythm, style, and volume all its own. It creates the atmosphere for every act and attraction; sets the stage as it were, builds and embellishes. It lends charm and gives class to performers; thrills, amuses and entertains patrons, and keeps the whole show together like one big family.

The band is primarily brass and the tempo very fast, like race horses breaking from the barrier or coming down the stretch; it keeps the show moving.

Each member of the band must have a strong lip and be master of his instrument--clarinet, trombone, saxophone, cornet, baritone, bass, percussions (drums) or French horns and sometimes even violins.

The band leader ties the entire program together in color, using the golden strands of sound to make an attractive package of entertainment and thrills lasting a rigid two hours and twenty minutes from the beginning of the opening spec (spectacular) to the end of the blow-off which sends the crowd home satisfied and happy.

When Merle Evans first joined "The Greatest Show on Earth" in that spring of 1919, he brought with him stacks of music he'd played as band leader on the 101 Wild West Show and had accumulated in ten years of trouping with circuses, carnivals, and other entertainment ventures.

He also had a choice of music written by such noted circus composers as Charles E. Duble, Frederick Jewell, J. J. Richards, Karl L. King, Walter English, Al Sweet, Henry Fillmore, and many others.

He knew he would need a staggering collection. Working feverishly, he assembled a score book of two hundred and twenty-six selections, each chosen to fit a particular act or attraction, each timed to quarter beat precision. His band must respond to these cues and emergency cut-ins. It must go with split-second rapidity from waltzes to galops, marches to quadrilles, never an instant too early or too late.

Evans, perfectionist that he always has been, wrote a great deal of his own circus music, holding and fingering his cornet with his right hand while scribbling with his left, a big bowl of pop corn within easy reach. Much of his composing was done at night on the circus train, after he'd played and led the band for seven hours for two shows and concerts plus the street parade.

"We didn't use many of the pieces I wrote on the show because I didn't want people to say I just played my own stuff," he explains.

One of his most popular numbers was "Fredella," written for his friends, Fred and Ella Bradna, the "general equestrian director" and the noted equestrienne.

Merle also wrote "Red Wagons," "Symphonia," "Fanfare" and many more marches, smears, galops and quadrilles. He cut ten albums under such labels as Columbia, RCA, Everett, Capitol, Crest, and Century. Most of his records are now collector's items because the real old-time circus band is only a memory, but he recently cut a new Crest album and now is considering an album of Sousa marches.

"If I had to assemble a circus band tomorrow," Merle says, "I wouldn't know where to start. There just aren't many musicians to play circus music any more. They're just not around."

In the old days the circus carried its own band and there were other experienced musicians among performers and even workingmen. However, beginning in the 1940s and 1950s the band leader and his drummer, Red Floyd, and organist Bob Boucher, recruited local musicians and paid union scale.

"I'd rehearse them for maybe two hours before the first show and we'd be ready to go," he explains. "We'd usually get the same musicians year after year in each town we played. Some were good and some not so good.

"As long as a musician gave it all he had, I'd put up with him. The two things I could not abide and still don't like are putting something into the music that isn't there—not written in—and drinking on the job.

"The exactness of the circus makes drinking and carousing impossible. I would never allow a drinking man to play in my band. If I caught him at it, he'd be paid off at once and dismissed. I don't drink or smoke myself, and I don't think I could have stood the strain of my work, day after day, if I did.

"I guess I fired more drunken musicians than anybody else in the world. I just would not tolerate a drinking musician."

#	RING 1	STAGE 1	RING 2	STAGE 2	RING 3
1	TIGERS		BEARS		LEOPARDS
2	MILLETTE	ZOPPE	LA NORMA	ROBBINS	TRISKA
3			LEAPS		
			CLOWN WASHING MACHINE		
4	ZOPPE		GUISTINO LOYAL CUCCIOLI		BOSTOCK SEIFERT
5			GUTIS		
6			**** BIRTHDAY "SPEC" ****		
7			GERALDOS		
8	ASIA BOYS		BRUNN		FRANKLIN & ASTRID
		*****	CLOWNS - CLOWNS *****		
9	DOBRITCH	clowns	ROLA - ROLA		JOANIDIES
10	KAY BURSLEM	GIRL IN MOON	ALMA PIAIA	GIRL IN MOON	JEAN SLEETER

#				
13			UNUS	
14	ELEPHANTS		CLOWN CAR	ELEPHANTS
15	DEL MORALS		C L O W N S	
16	MULES		LOS ONAS	2 JACKS
			PETERSON'S JOCKEY DOG	CHIMPANZEES	PONIES
	C L O W N C R A Z Y N U M B E R			
17	FLYING ACT		FLYING ACT	FLYING ACT
			C L O W N S	
18	CLAUDE VALOIS	SAN FRANCISCO	LILLIAN WITTMACK SAN FRANCISCO	CILLY FEINDT
19			CLOWN NUMBER "SCHOOL DAZE"	
20	ROMANOS	ROBENIS	BOKARAS	BOGINOS
21			JACOBS CLOWN CAR	
22			ALZANAS	
23		************	F I N A L E ************	

Typical cue sheet used by Merle Evans

In his head Merle carried a fantastic collection of music and could recall instantly any number he wished. He still does. Friends often gave him music, some of it never recorded, and some going back into the last century.

One collection came from Fred Daw, Sr., a Chicago entertainer and father of Freddie the Clown. Daw and his partner once tried out for the Amos 'n Andy radio show but lost out to another pair named Freeman Gosden and Charles Correll. Their show was immensely popular in the 1920s and 1930s.

"Very few people realize the importance of music in a circus," Merle says. "In a single performance our band had to provide more than 200 music cues, actually representing that many different compositions.

"Some of them were mere fanfares; others might be brief excerpts of a certain rhythmic type. But there also were many complete pieces ranging from old-fashioned waltzes to galops to elaborate production numbers and classics of the world's great music.

"I put all this material into a single book I made up before the season started, and gave each player a copy. Naturally, the repertoire changed some from year to year, but there's some music that simply can't be changed. That's because human and animal performers have become so accustomed to it that any variation would upset their acts.

"It's fair to say that trained horses in particular are very dependent on musical cues. The same thing can be said of elephants, big cats, and bears. A trapeze artist, aerialist or a balancing act must have just the right music, in a perfect and familiar rhythm. If not, something could go wrong; their timing would be off.

"The tempo of every performance under the Big Top was set by the circus band. We played for the center ring if there was a choice, but practically every participant in the show developed musical likes and dislikes. I mean habits that spelled consistent success. We had to look for these.

"And in case of accident, we had to be ready with some emergency music. We never knew when it might be needed. I still think a good many circus fans don't realize the skill and training that must go into a lot of acts. Performers must be in top physical condition because their acts are timed to the fraction of a second. The band must stay in shape, too.

"While the so-called lower animals unquestionably respond to definite music cues, especially a change of pace or finish of an act, it would be an exaggeration to say they actually keep time to a musical beat, as humans do.

"Usually when a society horse appears to be dancing or walking rhythmically, it's the band that is keeping time with the animal.

"Our concert numbers usually included such favorites as 'The Golden Dragon,' 'Royal Decree,' 'Rolling Thunder,' and selections from the classics by Rossini, Liszt, Auber, Wagner, Friml, Herbert, and Verdi.

"One of the most famous musical pieces traditionally associated with the circus is 'Entrance of the Gladiators," also known as 'Thunder and Blazes.' My band actually made four recordings of this lively and familiar piece.

"There was a time when Waldteufel's 'Skaters' Waltz' was considered ideal for a trapeze act, and we also made a lot of use of John T. Hall's 'Wedding of the Winds.' Later we used Paul Lincke's 'Spring, Beautiful Spring." He's the man who wrote 'Glow Worm.'

"Karl King, my predecessor, wrote a number of excellent marches, one of which he called 'Barnum & Bailey's Favorite.' We played it many times. Most of the fan fares were my own. I also contributed some marches but, as I said, I didn't play too much of my own music because I didn't want to be criticized, you see?

"A breakdown of the music for one of our programs a few years ago shows some interesting contrasts and comparisons. It's a mixture of the old and the new, the popular and the classic.

"The opening animal act demanded some Oriental music such as the Rimsky-Korsakoff 'Song of India,' plus a 'March to Mecca' and 'Caravan Club.' But when it was time for the cats to scramble back to their quarters, we naturally played the old 'Tiger Rag' and every striped beauty seemed to welcome the familiar sounds.

"What we called the 'Little Aerial' was accompanied by such music as 'Mr. Sandman,' Gershwin's 'Sewanee,' the Youmans 'Hallelujah' and Irving Berlin's 'No Business Like Show Business.' A boisterous bit of baseball burlesque by the clowns naturally called for 'Take Me out to the Ball Game.'

"Then we had a combination of tight and slack wire acts with Spanish artists and we saluted them with things like 'Valencia,' 'Say Si Si' and the tango, 'La Cumparsita.'

"Dogs, monkeys and ponies appear to like a fast two-four time. We gave them the Karl King march, a 'Broadway Two-Step' and a couple of pieces called 'Walking Frog' and 'Kentucky Sunrise.'

"The first production number in the show one year had the title, 'On Honolulu Bay,' with music by John Ringling North and lyrics by Irving Caesar, This included the theme song of the 1955 'Greatest Show on Earth' modestly called 'Impossible.'

"Incidentally, John Ringling North is a good musician, an excellent musician. He plays saxophone. He's written such popular numbers as

'Lovely Luawana Lady,' with lyrics by E. Ray Goetz. North's even a member of ASCAP.

"Now, for the trained horses we had what we call the 'Liberty Act' and used a combination of marches and fan fares. Here's where we played one of my own compositions, 'Symphonia,' which I wrote for Charles Ringling in 1926. Charles Ringling also was an excellent musician and his son, Robert, studied with Enrico Caruso and sang in the Chicago Opera Company.

"We got the Liberty horses back to their positions at the end of their act with the 'Eclipse Gallop.' During a roping and whip-cracking performance we played 'Red River Valley,' 'Home on the Range,' Cole Porter's 'Don't Fence Me In,' and the Katchaturian 'Sabre Dance.'

"Another type of horsemanship known as 'dressage' calls for special music. The horses go through these intricate maneuvers and riders control them by slight movement of hands, legs and weight. We played numbers like 'Espano,' 'Carioca' and 'The Donkey Serenade.'

"For a bit of clowning, we played 'Muskrat Ramble' and a Victor Herbert waltz elevated a high wire performance. Later we played Herbert's 'March of the Toys.' Another North-Caesar production number was called 'Holidays' and we used it to climax the first part of the show.

"For Unus, the acrobat who balanced on one finger atop a small globe, we used the current hit, 'Melody of Love,' Glenn Miller's theme, 'Sunrise Serenade,' Peter DeRose's 'Deep Purple' and 'Awakening of Spring' by a fellow named Bach. Incidentally, this Unus was a great showman.

"Victor Young's 'The Greatest Show on Earth,' written for the movie of the same name, featured the flying trapeze act while acrobats tumbled to the tune, 'Circus Echoes,' written by Arthur Hughes, who used to play the calliope.

"Every act is done to counts. Acrobats steady themselves to it, jugglers get in the groove and aerialists time their swings, downdrops, leaps and hand contacts to it.

"The drum roll builds tension and keeps the senses alert. But when suspense reaches its crest and the climactic moment is at hand, the drummer ceases his roll and muffles the snares. When the artist completes a difficult backward somersault the band hits a triumphant smear.

"For several seasons we accompanied Lillian Leitzel with the 'Crimson Petal Waltz' but after she fell to her death in 1931, I put away her favorites and never played 'Crimson Petal' or 'Hungarian Rhapsody No. 2' at a circus performance again. I consider this Leitzel's own music."

Some other numbers are considered jinxes and Evans wouldn't think of playing them. One of these is Von Suppe's "Light Cavalry March."

One time Evans' circus band played it in Oklahoma and a train wreck two days later killed sixteen circus folk. A year or so later, he tried the same number on the 101 Wild West Show. A blowdown followed and thirty-eight persons died. The third time he used it, a cornet player dropped dead just as the performance ended.

"Well, that was enough for me," Merle recalls. "I had all the parts gathered up and destroyed. It was enough for me. Three times and out."

As band director at every circus performance, Merle Evans had to keep his eyes on the rings and stages so he always stood with his back to the musicians, leading with his left hand and playing cornet with his right. Thus he could watch performers in the three rings and aloft, timing each act's music to the split second.

He also had to sense disaster and try to forestall it. The band's job was not only to bring out the spirit and finesse of every act but be alert for a possible accident, fire, or blowdown.

"If a wind threatened to blow our tents down, we had to be ready," Merle says. "If the lions got nasty, a trapeze performer took a spill or rigging slipped, it was up to us. We had to cut right off in the middle of a waltz or a fox trot or whatever and go into a familiar tune.

"This quick change seemed to soothe the nerves of troupers and patrons alike. After that we'd slip into a slightly faster melody and the show carried on as if nothing had happened---without a break in the music, too.

"I arranged seating so none of my musicians had to turn his own music. You see, I had the men play alternate strains so one temporarily idle could turn for his neighbor. It worked just fine.

"On the original Ringling-Barnum show, after they combined, the band gave a thirty-minute concert in the center ring before each performance. With the show itself, this meant playing nearly seven hours a day, so any little thing to save time or energy was appreciated.

"We mentioned the motion picture, 'The Greatest Show on Earth,' which was a good one and made a lot of money. Well, some of it was filmed at Sarasota and my band played for the parade scenes. But we didn't come out too well, financially. Twice I had to say 'Okay' to Betty Hutton, the star, and each time I got paid fifty-six dollars."

Imported acts sometimes gave the band leader a bit of trouble, but he usually solved any differences through diplomacy. Once a group of Chinese tumblers insisted on Western music for their act. They just liked the tune.

Merle obliged but the act lost all its zip and appeal. He quickly pointed this out. The tumblers asked what he'd suggest. He resurrected two ancient tunes called "Fantan" and "In Old Pekin." The acrobats liked his choice and their act improved so much they turned completely against Western Music.

"Some foreign acts brought their own music and if I found it acceptable, we'd use it. But the choice was always up to me. As a rule, they'd say 'We'll leave the music up to you,' and I'd use my own judgment. They were generally agreeable.

"But I remember one act, a teeterboard troupe from Europe, brought its own music. They gave it to me and I played it. But the manager of another troupe in the next ring hollered bloody murder and he says to me, 'If that Hungarian music is played, my people won't work.'

" 'Hungarian?' I says. 'Who told you that? It's not Hungarian at all. That music's pure Spanish, from Madrid."

" 'Okay,' the manager grinned and bowed his apologies. 'Spanish. Okay. Está bien!'

"Of course he never knew the difference."

10

The Grandest Show on Earth

To millions of fans throughout America, thousands of troupers, and to Merle Evans himself, there never was anything like the Ringling Bros. and Barnum & Bailey Combined Circus of 1919 and a score or more years afterward.

It traveled aboard ninety-two and later one hundred railroad cars in four trains, touring more than 15,000 miles a season and giving more than four hundred performances in well over a hundred cities and towns coast to coast, border to border, and in Canada.

"Anybody who never saw the Ringling show in the 1920s doesn't have any idea what he missed," says the band leader with conviction. "We had everything---a complete city in itself. There was nothing we needed that wasn't available, right on the lot.

"Why, they even had a commissary wagon, parked right beside the cook house. You could buy shoes, socks, cigarettes, candy bars, tooth paste---even postage stamps! You could get anything you needed.

"We had two barbers---regular barbers they were, and good ones. They traveled with the show. Every morning they'd set up their two chairs and make hot water for shaves. In those days every man got his shaves at the barber shop. We paid, I think, a quarter for a haircut.

"The Big Top was, I think, about 240 feet wide by 520 feet long. Why, the canvas alone, just for the main tent, weighed I'm told twenty tons dry. Imagine what it weighed after a heavy rain!

"The canvas alone, with the menagerie tent, side show tents, dressing tents, cook tent and the rest covered something like fifteen acres of ground.

"The show carried 125 cooks and waiters; baked all our pies and cakes and served around 4,500 meals a day. We had our own blacksmith shop, light plants, hospital car---the whole works.

"We had 350 head of baggage horses, in the days before motor power took over---big draft horses, Percherons and Clydesdales. We had 150 head of performing horses and 40 ponies on the show; we used thousands of tons of hay on the tour, just to feed the animals.

"We had 52 bulls---all elephants are called bulls on the show. Bert Partridge, George Denman, and Fred Baker were in charge of them, and of course they had helpers.

"We used elephants to help move wagons on and off the lot. Crowds used to gather to see us unload; see the wagons rolling off the flats and all the wild animals being hauled off to the circus grounds. Being an early riser, I liked to watch it myself.

"It was a real treat for a lot of people, to see us unload and set up. In those days, the circus was always the biggest thing in town. People never tired of watching us turn fifteen acres of weeds, grass, and sand into a fairyland.

"It took a lot of horses and elephants, tractors and trucks, men and sledge hammers; took a lot of poles, stakes, canvas, and guy ropes to build that city, and tear it down.

"Sometimes it would take a couple of days to make a run, like the 721 miles from North Kansas City to Denver and the 718 miles from Portland to San Francisco, the 646 from El Paso to Dallas, and the 626 from Denver to Salt Lake City.

"Usually we'd make a jump from one town to the next overnight, and our shortest move was the ten miles from Minneapolis to St. Paul.

"The first train would begin to load about 5:30 p.m., and by 10:30 would be ready to roll. It would include personnel and equipment of the cookhouse, commissary, horseshoeing, harnessmaking, and blacksmith departments; menagerie tent and wild animals; trucks, tractors, floats, ticket wagons, and office wagon.

"The second section included the Big Top and most other tents, pole and stake wagons, working elephants, light and sanitation departments; tractors, trucks and diesel plants. It was usually loaded and ready to move at 2 a.m.

"The third section was loaded as soon as the first section pulled out, but it always left after the second section. It carried the performing elephants, horses, ponies, camels, and zebras; trainers, hostlers, and grooms; 39 wagons including the wardrobe wagons and band wagon.

"The fourth and last section included big show and side show performers, band men, executives, and office personnel. It was ready to leave any time after the third section departed and was made up of state room and Pullman sleepers.

"By the time we'd get in, the cook tent would be up and breakfast ready. The food was marvelous, just marvelous. We'd have juices, cereals, eggs and bacon, sausage or ham; toast, hot cakes and gallons of coffee, tea or milk.

"Here's a food order for one day:

"Fresh meat 2,470 pounds, 276 dozen eggs, 2,220 loaves of bread, 285 pounds of butter, 30 gallons of milk, 1,300 pounds of fresh vegetables, 200 pounds of coffee and tea, 110 dozen oranges, 50 bushels of potatoes, 3,600 ears of fresh corn (if available), and two barrels of sugar.

"Breakfast would run until 8:30 or 9 o'clock, then the cook house would open up for lunch at 11:30 so all could eat before the matinee crowd started coming in.

"Under normal conditions, side show performers and the eight musicians in the Wild West band would have dinner about 3:30 in the afternoon. Each was allowed 45 minutes to eat, get back to his place, and catch the blow-off.

"When the show was over, all of us left would be performers and musicians. This would be around 4:30 or 5 o'clock, and we'd run over and get our dinner.

"If you were a slow eater, they'd pull the checkered tablecloths right out from under you, or even take the table. They're in a hurry to pack up and get into the next town, you see? "

Merle and his band played not only for all performances, and sometimes there were three on Saturdays and holidays, but in the concert and street parade. The band leader would put groups of music makers between displays all along the two-mile procession. Circus press agents called this "A winding, dazzling river of silver and gold mixed with music."

Flag bearers and four buglers marched at the head of the parade, following the outrider's warning cry, "Hold your horses! Here it comes!"

Next came the bagpipe band to attract attention with the reedy stuff. A short distance behind was Merle Evans and his eighteen-piece band, riding in the great Two Hemispheres band wagon drawn by eight matched horses, their harness and trappings glittering in the sun.

"Pat Valdo and Charlie Bell, two well-known clowns, would play cornet in the clown band," Merle says. "Then we had the side show band, a fine black band under P. G. Lowery. He was an excellent cornet player and the first black to graduate from the New England Conservatory of Music.

"We had ten camels pulling the Deegan Uniphone wagon. Then we'd have the usher's band, the ticket seller's band, and finally the elephants and two calliopes bringing up the rear.

"These were actually a variation of the organ, or piano. We jokingly called them 'steam fiddles' or 'steam pianos.' Our old steam calliope weighed around seven thousand pounds. It had a boiler but ran out of steam quite often, so they'd have to fire up and make more steam.

"The calliope has no range but, Christ, you can hear one for miles. The one we had on the old *Cotton Blossom* was hooked up to the boiler, so we had plenty of steam. You could hear us five or ten miles up and down the river and out into the swamps.

"I always liked the calliope but never learned to play one very well. They get out of tune in wet weather but they never missed drawing the crowds. There aren't too many of them around any more, except in Museums.

"There's a man in Jacksonville, Florida, who used to repair them for the show; replace broken parts and replace whistles. He's sort of an authority on calliopes, his name is Tommy White.

"These parades were no picnics to us, whether walking or riding in heavy, cumbersome wagons over cobblestone streets in hot sun, rain, wind, or cold. But they were all part of the job and helped whip up enthusiasm for the show.

"If it looked like rain, we's take along raincoats to protect ourselves and instruments. If it rained, we couldn't play the snare drum because

The big Liberty bandwagon of Ringling Bros. and Barnum & Bailey circus

the head would burst. So we'd take along a bucket and we'd turn it upside down and bang on it; it worked just fine.

"The parades could be hazardous to musicians in cities like Boston and Kansas City especially. They had some bad hills in Kansas City in those days. We had a driver and two helpers to keep the horses and the old Two Hemispheres band wagon under control, or try to.

"They'd put on brake shoes but even then that old wagon would go swinging down the hill, threatening to turn over any minute. The brakes would squeak and smoke and the horses would rear and prance, trying to find footing or get away from the heavy single-trees banging on their legs. Oh, we had some scary times on that old wagon."

Back on the lot, an experienced crew of executives and assistants kept the circus on its tight schedule. There were managers and superintendents of the numerous departments and divisions like a well-run city---a vast, complex yet coordinated operation in which every man had a job to do.

The show carried thirty porters, under a superintendent. The head of the ice department was properly uniformed, and had two helpers. The department of sanitation had a superintendent and several helpers. They looked after the "donnickers"---some spell it "donagher"---those little enclosures in inconspicuous places marked "Men" and "Women."

"People called putting up and taking down 'The Second Greatest Show on Earth' and it was," Merle agrees. "The railroad sidings would be maybe half a mile or maybe five miles from the lot. Horses and elephants walked it. We rode in three personnel buses. Everything else was carried from the train to the grounds and back again by truck or wagon.

"The lot superintendent, using a measuring tape, would lay out where the tents were to go long before canvas men, elephants, and stake drivers moved in to raise them.

"One by one the 39 tents of various sizes would mushroom to the rhythm of a sing-song chant by burly canvas men, the steady thud of sledge hammers and great pulling power of elephants. The Big Top lived up to its name. It was 38,500 yards of canvas hoisted on 186 poles including five Oregon fir poles 62 feet long, costing $1,800 apiece.

"We had about 200 wagons in those days, each designed for a special function. We had five water tank trucks holding 1,000 gallons each to supply the cookhouse, performers, workingmen, and animals. This was the only item except food we brought in.

"By 10 or 10:30 o'clock we'd be set up and ready for the parade. The veterinary doctor would be checking animals, the blacksmith shoeing horses, barbers cutting hair, nurses treating cuts, sprains and bruises, women in the wardrobe top unloading costumes and putting them all in place—everything had to be just right when the show went on, you see?

"Over in the Big Top, there'd be a crew of electricians and prop men stringing wires and putting in lights and rigging. Another crew would cover the ground with fresh sawdust.

"On good days many would do their laundry in the back yard, and use guy ropes as clothes lines while their children played hide and seek among the wagons. Most of us, if we were in town more than one day, had laundry and dry cleaning done commercially.

"By the middle of the morning, the circus mailman had come from the post office and was giving out the mail. Getting cards and letters from friends was always a bright spot in our busy, crowded day.

"The whole operation was just great, geared to efficiency and coordination; fascinating to watch. In bright, warm weather on dry lots life was easy and pleasant. But even in rain or snow, heat or cold, we moved with the same speed and determination for the show must go on."

11

Two Brothers Ringling

Charles and John Ringling were about as far apart in character and personality as two brothers in the same undertaking could be. Fortunately, they were seldom together after they grew up and their differences offset each other when they were.

All those in personnel called the warm, friendly and considerate older brother "Mr. Charlie" and the stubborn, cold and calculating one "Mr. John." They approved, for one did not wish to be mistaken for the other.

To those outside the big circus family, "Mr. Ringling" meant John, a Titan among the minnows; front man, promoter, and a recognized wheeler-dealer.

While John and his first wife, Mable, lived aboard their private railroad car, the *Jomar*, some of the time, he came to the circus only occasionally and seldom set foot in the back yard. Thus he missed most of the headaches.

John and Mable traveled extensively in this country and abroad. He stayed up most of the night and didn't get up until after noon. If he happened to be in town, he might drop in on the circus, to check on it, perhaps to drop a few words of criticism, and pick up some cash. That was all.

"But he was class all the way," says Merle Evans, the band leader who worked for him for fifteen years. "You'd always know when he got to the show. He'd come in wearing those alligator shoes, two hundred and fifty-dollar suits, silk shirts, Homburg hat, and carrying a cane. He was real class; you bet.

"Everybody knew him; why, he was 'Mr. Big.' He chummed with such men as Al Smith, Harry Daugherty, Jim Farley, Mayor Frank (Boss) Hague of Jersey City, Mayor Jimmy Walker of New York; Henry

L. Doherty, Tex Rickard, Will Rogers, Col. Jacob Ruppert, John J. McGraw, and Sam Gumpertz.

"I've got a picture of John Ringling with nine of his friends, all millionaires. Imagine that? Ten millionaires all in one picture, in the days when a million dollars was a lot of money.

"Charles and his wife, Miss Edith, traveled a good deal with the show every year. They'd ride in their private car, the *Caledonia,* with the circus or to their homes in Evanston, Illinois, or Sarasota, Florida. They had two children, Hester and Robert. Hester was married to Charlie Sanford and living in Sarasota; Robert was at school in Chicago.

"Charles had some building and developing projects going on in Sarasota; had some real estate and a bank. But John was the big operator. He had a home in Alpine, New Jersey, and a New York apartment, but his big deals were in Sarasota. He had a lot of beach property and other real estate; had a fine home and was building a museum. John also had a bank.

"He had a lot of things going---railroads, oil wells, mines, ranch land---all over the country. But in the end very few of them paid off.

"When the depression struck in the late 1920s, Charlie had died and Mrs. Edith was running her bank. I'm told she paid off all claims when it closed. John's bank also closed but it didn't pay off.

"Mr. Charlie and his wife were real troupers; knew all the performers and most workingmen. They took a personal interest in the show and the people who made it go.

"He sure was a nice man. He'd come around and talk to everybody, right in the back yard. He spent a lot of time with the show although he was a busy man and had a lot of things going.

"He would come in and sit on the ring curb and hear us play those overtures. He was never critical, like John; always wanted a good band on the show. The two brothers would argue something awful! Charles was small but John was over six feet.

"I'll tell you how John Ringling was. He would see some alto players and they'd stop and he'd say to me, 'I'm paying those guys to play and they're not playing. Make 'em play.' He wanted them and all the others in the band to play every minute---blow your brains out, for his money.

"Miss Edith had a special uniform made for me. It was a gaudy thing, with a lot of gold leather on it; enough braid to outfit a dozen Navy admirals. I always wore it when she was around. She and Mr. Charlie thought a lot of me, and I liked them.

"We on the show never knew when the brothers might drop in. Charles and his wife would travel with us for several days or weeks, then leave. But John might pop in one night and be gone next day.

"Once I met Mr. Charlie on the street in Milwaukee. I was walking down the street and he saw me. He was in his limousine and had the chauffeur stop the car. He called me over.

"He says to me, 'Merle, how'd you like to go to Sarasota and play concert this winter? I says, 'Mr. Ringling, I'd like to but I've still got a year to go on that Bertram Mills contract in London.'

"He says, 'Oh, I'll take care of that. Give me your price tomorrow. We'll work it out.'

"So I gave him my price and he fixed it up with Mills, and that's how I first went to Sarasota, in 1925. I played with the concert band that winter. This was a nice little town; most of the people were very civic-minded. Our concerts always drew big crowds.

"Later I played at St. Petersburg; had a fine band over there. They called it the 'Merle Evans Sunshine City Band' and it was a good band, excellent band.

"Charles Ringling was always interested in music and he wanted plenty of it on the circus; always wanted a good band. He played violin and baritone. All the Ringlings were musicians. John played alto in the early days, on what we called a 'rain catcher,' and Alf T. helped Charles compose music for some of the early spectacles, such as 'Joan of Arc,' 'Cleopatra,' and others.

"I guess Otto was the only one not really a musician, but when they started trouping as 'Ringling Bros. Classic and Comic Concert Co.' in 1882, Otto beat the drum.

"Mr. Ringling---Charles that is---liked to play with the band once a season. He had a gold baritone, a gift from the Conn Company. We'd hear him practicing in the *Caledonia* and I'd tell my men 'get ready. Here comes 'Down on the Farm.' That was one of his favorites---that and 'The Lost Chord.'

"The day he was ready, he'd say to me, 'Merle, I'm ready,' and would come in and I'd put my cap on his bald head. Then he'd play, with band accompaniment. That would take care of him for the season.

"He always wanted a good band on the circus. We talked about it in 1926 and if he'd lived, the show would have come out with a 45-piece band for the 1927 season.

"Mr. Charlie also played violin very well. He had two Stradivarius, worth $30,000 apiece.

"He was at his home in Sarasota when he died on December 3, 1926. I remember it was the night Silas Green's show was playing Bradenton. I knew Charles Collier, the manager, and went up there to see him.

"When I got back to the hotel where I was staying, there was a note for me to call Eddie Rooney. I called and he told me Mr. Ringling had passed away. It was a shock and I sure was sorry.

"They had a big funeral for him. I was a pallbearer, along with Eddie Rooney and Ed Norwood, the press agent. I don't remember the others, but the lieutenant governor of Illinois was there. They buried Mr. Ringling in Manasota Park, up between Sarasota and Bradenton.

"John Ringling wasn't at his brother's funeral. I don't know where he was---probably in New York or Europe, buying art or looking for bargains; maybe hunting circus acts. John was always traveling, making deals.

"He liked big animals, like sea elephants and gorillas; sensational acts and big drawing cards. Once he bought a gorilla named John Daniel for $30,000. This gorilla had been raised in a home and didn't like being caged up. He was a big hit but didn't live very long.

"Mr. John got another gorilla but this didn't last long, either. None of 'em did, until Johnny North bought Gargantua and put him in a specially-built air conditioned cage. I guess he got the idea for the gorilla from his old Uncle John.

"Then there was Mademoiselle Toto; we got her from Cuba, from Mrs. Marie Hoyt. Johnny North was there at the time, to close the deal with Mrs. Hoyt, and persuade her to let the gorilla come to the circus. I'm not sure what sort of deal it was, but she came with the gorilla, and stayed with her.

"Paul Danovsky brought the gorilla to Port Everglades by boat and then across the state by train to Sarasota. That's when they had the 'wedding'---Gargantua and Toto---in the winter of 1941. You were there; wasn't that something? Swarms of people jammed in and around the tent where they held this wedding.

"Danovsky says you should see the mahogany furniture Mrs. Hoyt had for Toto, embedded in concrete so she couldn't throw it around. And she had a sound system in the gorilla's room so she could hear what went on day or night.

"Roland Butler got a picture and painted breasts on it; great big things. Toto didn't have any more tits than old Gargantua did. Anyhow, Mrs. Hoyt was a high-class woman. Jose Tomas was Toto's keeper and Richard Kroener had charge of Gargantua. Both had lived with the gorillas for years. When Kroener died, Tomas was in charge of the gorilla crew.

"Mrs. Hoyt bought Tomas a white Cadillac with red leather upholstery. She was a fine woman; stayed with Toto until the gorilla died just a few years ago. Then Mrs. Hoyt passed away.

"Mr. John was always afraid of somebody getting hurt; he didn't like claims for damages. I remember once we had some swinging ladders---we called 'em the 'chambermaid's frolic.' We had about thirty of these swinging ladders and the girls would sail around the arena and out over the hippodrome track.

"They were spectacular but John didn't like 'em at all. Every time he'd come on the show and see those ladders, he'd get hot and say, 'Take them out.' So we'd take 'em out and the minute he left, we'd put them right back.

"It was a beautiful act and we'd play a waltz while the girls in their pretty dresses swung around the arena; a beautiful act. But Mr. John didn't like it and he wanted those ladders out of there.

"The show moved winter quarters to Sarasota from Bridgeport in 1927---after Mr. Charlie died---and stayed there until 1959. Then Art Concello, who was general manager at the time, moved it down to Venice. I think that's the only mistake Art Concello ever made in his life. He should have kept it in Sarasota.

"One year Mr. John was aboard the *Jomar* at winter quarters. It was the middle of March and we hadn't made any plans, so I called on him. I wanted to know about the band---we were due to open in two weeks. Here we were, almost time to head for New York and I hadn't heard a word about the band. That's the way he was---put off everything 'til the last minute.

"So I went out to the winter quarters and he says to me, 'Merley'---he always called me 'Merley.' He says, 'What about the band?'

" 'Well, Mr. John,' I says, 'What about it?' 'Well,' he says, 'Merley, hire eight trombones and eight cornets and two drummers.' That's all he wanted, just a lot of power.

"I says, 'Mr. John, you can't play anything with that. You've got to have clarinets; you've got to have brass. You've got no foundation for a circus band.'

"Well, he hee-hawed around there for ten or fifteen minutes and we talked and argued a little. Finally he says, 'Oh, go ahead and use what you had last year.' That's the way he was.

"John and Sam Gumpertz had been friends for years and were in some promotions together. Then they became bitter enemies. You see, John had over-reached himself when he bought the American Circus Corporation in 1929, just before the crash. Then the depression came on. John couldn't meet his notes and the bondholders put Gumpertz in charge.

"John Ringling was listed as circus president, but he had no authority on or off the lot. It got so John and Gumpertz wouldn't speak to each other. And Gumpertz was the boss. That really hurt John.

"The last time I saw him he came on the show in Brooklyn with his nurse. Gumpertz had given orders, so Pat Valdo told me, that he didn't want anybody to talk to Mr. John.

"Well, when the show was over I saw him sitting in a chair across the way, so I went right across the center ring and talked with him a few minutes. That was on the lot in Brooklyn in the spring of 1936. It was the last time I ever saw John Ringling.

"As far as I know, he never came on the lot again. He died that December, in his New York apartment. Even so, he was the only one of the bunch to live to be 70 years of age, and he just made it with about six months to spare.

"When I saw him the last time, he'd had a stroke and dragged his leg when he walked. He had to use a cane. John had always carried a cane for show but he needed it then. It was depressing to see a man go down like he did.

"The only time I ever saw Alf T. was when he came on the show in that 1919 season, right after they combined. I remember they took out a couple of sections of seats so they could drive his Rolls Royce in. They sent word he wanted to meet me, so I went over and shook hands with him. He died that fall, October, so of the brothers I only knew Charles and John well.

"I'll tell you another thing about John Ringling. He was a fantastic eater. Oh, how he could put the groceries away! All the Ringlings were big eaters but I guess John could out-do any of the others at the dinner table. He loved to eat.

"John Staley, who worked for the Ringlings and later ran the cookhouse on the Clyde Beatty show, can tell you about John's appetite. He says John was a terrific eater; had breakfast when he got up about 1 o'clock in the afternoon---a big one.

"They tell me when he had that Japanese cook, Willy Susa, he'd get up and have a big slug of special mineral water as a starter. Then he'd tear into a big bowl of fresh fruit. Willy would take four or five grapefruit, maybe some oranges, apples, bananas, pineapples, peaches, and pears and cut them all up. He'd add maybe a few grapes and mix the whole thing up in a big bowl.

"John Ringling would eat the whole thing. Then he'd be all set for a hearty breakfast! And he'd drink coffee with the caffeine taken out. His cigars also had the nicotine out. He had the best Havanas.

"But of all the Ringlings I knew and worked for, I'll say Mr. Charlie was the nicest. He was a very nice man; a lot smaller physically than

John---actually rather tiny---but a nice man. None of us on the show ever got close to Mr. John except Fred Bradna, who used to eat and drink with him.

"Bradna used to go over to John's house, Ca d' Zan, after his second wife, Emily, left him, and keep him company. Bradna said John would drink about a dozen pints of that imported beer he always had on hand. Then he'd eat two or three roast chickens before he turned in. This would be around 4 or 5 o'clock in the morning, and he'd always sleep 'til after noon.

"The Ringlings weren't all stone-hearted, and even John had a streak of goodness in him. After old Yankee Robinson died, they and the Sells brothers put up a nice monument over his grave in the city cemetery at Jefferson, Iowa, where he died late in that summer of 1884.

"I'll tell you another little story about John Ringling. We had a clown named Fred Snelling, a terrific clown. He had a whip with a butterfly on it. One day they found his body in the gutter in Philadelphia and put it in a pauper's grave; thought he was some old bum.

"John Ringling heard about it and he had the body taken up and put in a very nice cemetery, with proper services, too.

"I think it's ironical that John's body was never put in that crypt in the museum he built. Most of the Ringlings are buried in Baraboo---Alf T. and his wife were buried in New York state. But John and Mable's bodies are still in New Jersey; they never got to the crypt they'd built.

"Not long ago someone suggested in the paper that Sarasota put up a monument to John Ringling for what he did for the city. I think it's a swell idea; I'd go for that."

12

Ups and Downs on the Big Show

Merle Evans talks the way he plays cornet, with verve and finality; in a staccato spiel that leaps from one sentence to the next, part in the present tense and part in the past. His voice rises and falls like his music, from a mellow tone to a strident trill, in sureness and happy recollections.

His clear, bright blue eyes sparkle and they're rimmed with lines of laughter that scramble all over his full, rounded face and reach down to his chin. He bubbles with good humor and the joy of being alive, among good friends, active and in perfect health despite his 77 years. Life to him has been full of hard work and happy experiences.

He likes to remember the Ringling Bros. and Barnum & Bailey Combined Circus as it was when he first joined up and for an exciting decade afterward, when the giant outdoor amusement enterprise was at its biggest and best.

"The show from the 1920s to about 1940 was great, just great," he says with a nostalgic sigh. "We had wonderful music, big attractions and thrilling acts---the very best. It was an excellent show, excellent show.

"John Ringling was in command for nearly ten years after his brother died, although he owned only a third of it. The others were Mrs. Edith Ringling and Mrs. Aubrey Ringling. Aubrey was the widow of Richard, who was Alf T.'s son. John Ringling was a good circus man; knew how to route the show and what he wanted. After Mr. Charlie died, he ran the show and it made a lot of money.

"Our performers were the greatest. You'll find them on any list of all-time greats. We had riders like May Wirth, Ella Bradna, Fred Derrick, Orrin Davenport, the Cristianis, Loyal-Repenskys, Dorothy Herbert, Bobby Steele, and Captain William Heyer.

"We had flyers like Alfredo Codona, Arthur and Antoinette

Merle Evans and his band under the Big Top in 1939

Uniforms for the 1940 season featured long coats and caps with floppy tops

Two of the circus' greatest press agents at work in the old press car at winter quarters in Sarasota, Florida, in 1943: Frank Braden (left) and Roland Butler

Concello, the Clarkonians; and of course, we had Leitzel. We had wire artists like Con and Winnie Colleano, Charlie Siegrist, and Fred Silbon.

"We had good clowns, too; a lot of excellent clowns. I would name Spader Johnson, Pat Valdo, Otto Griebling, Lou Jacobs, Paul Jerome, Paul Jung, Emmett Kelly, and Felix Adler---oh, a lot of them.

"After Mable Stark, we had such wild animal trainers as Frank Buck, Clyde Beatty, Alfred Court, and Terrell Jacobs. We even had Tom Mix, the movie star---we had the best of all of them;

"I'll tell you another thing I think everybody will agree with me on: We had the best press department any circus ever had, even in the old days. We had Dexter Fellows, Roland Butler, Frank Braden, Allen Lester, Gardner Wilson, Eddie Johnson, Bill Fields---all professionals; the very best.

"Dexter Fellows was probably the best known of 'em all until he passed away in Hattiesburg, Mississippi, in 1937. He was with Barnum & Bailey and left after the merger, then came back to us.

"Dexter had trouped for years. He'd show up in New York a couple of weeks ahead of the show, dressed fit to kill. He'd wear a straw skimmer or gray fedora perched at jaunty angle, and he'd have on a checkered vest with a gold watch chain stretched across the front. He always carried a gold-headed cane. Oh, he was a stylish fellow.

"Dexter would saunter into the news rooms of those New York papers and say 'hello' to his friends; he knew everybody and they knew him. Next day the papers would say something like, 'Spring arrived from Florida yesterday. Dexter Fellows just blew in to announce the circus will open as usual in Madison Square Garden.'

"Likely as not, the story would be on the front page, and a picture of Dexter with it. After that the papers would have ads and stories almost daily about the circus coming to town, with pictures of riders and elephants and clowns. It was great publicity for us.

"Frank Braden was a dapper little guy---always looked like a fashion model with his hat cocked to one side, starched cuffs with glittering gold cufflinks sticking out of his jacket sleeves. He was a very fancy dresser.

"Frank was a graduate of Annapolis and a cavalry officer in the Philippines. Quite a man, Braden was. He was the fellow responsible for that picture of the midget sitting on old J. P. Morgan's knee! It ran in newspapers everywhere.

"Roland Butler was head of the press department for over thirty years, and one of the greatest. Not only was he good with words but Roland was also an artist. He could sketch in oversize teeth, big lips, enormous ears and scary eyes so they'd look natural---like the real thing.

"He could make any animal look twice as ferocious as a hungry Russian bear. Study his stuff and you'd almost be afraid to troupe with such creatures. Oh, how he could build 'em up!

"He called Gargantua 'The mightiest monster ever captured by man;' 'Most fiendishly ferocious brute that breathes!' Under his expert hand and paint brush, Gargantua became the biggest attraction we ever had. I'd say he was on a par with Barnum's elephant, Jumbo.

"Gargy trouped with us over ten years. He was a tremendous attraction to the end. He hung on until right after the final performance in the 1949 season at Miami. Then he died before we went into winter quarters.

"All the others in the press car knew their stuff, too. They'd fan out over the country, calling on newspaper editors and talking with reporters and politicians in every city and town along the route and some not on it. We got a lot of front page publicity in those days.

"But we needed all of it. It cost $25,000 a day just to keep the show going.

"I never was much for gambling but in those days the workingmen would spread a blanket down beside the train, set a couple of lanterns on the ground and roll the dice. Craps was the popular game, and there was always a crap game going, right up until the train pulled out.

"It was a rugged life, but we loved it. Trouping was hard because you had a parade and a concert as well as playing for the performances. We played for about seven hours a day, six days a week; there were no Sunday shows then.

"On Sundays they'd wash all the wagons, clean up everything. The horses needed a rest, too, you see? And the performers. We could get our laundry done, maybe do some sightseeing if we weren't making a long jump, and get some rest.

"All my players had nicknames. I called the organ player 'Mule Train,' and I had a drummer we called 'Boom Boom.' We had another player we called 'Moose Face.' 'Shrimp Boat' was another. One fellow had the smallest snare drum I ever saw. We named him 'E-flat,'

"Oh, we had some real characters. One fellow named Frank Seavy was a cornet player. He had a drinking problem. After our last show that season he knew he wouldn't be back, so when we played 'Auld Lang Syne' he stepped down off the band stand and went over to a center pole near us. He wrapped that cornet right around the center pole, and left it there!"

13

The Strange People

While the circus band had no professional connection with what the public knew as the side show, strange people or "freaks," these happy humans were part of the big circus family when it traveled under canvas and many good and lasting friendships developed between them and the musicians, performers, and workingmen.

Generally it was billed as the "Congress of Freaks" but usually it was called "The Side Show" and in circus parlance it was the "The Kid Show."

The Ringling show usually had fifteen or twenty in the side show, including a sword swallower, fire eater, fat girl, world's tallest couple, snake handler, giant, human splinter, long-haired girl, and perhaps a comedy juggler and magician.

Lew Graham was side show manager for many years and so was Clyde Ingalls. Both were close friends of Merle Evans and the band leader took a liking to and personal interest in these strange people, among them Frieda Pushnik, the armless and legless girl who trouped with the show for many years.

An illustration of the comradeship that often developed on the circus, is the case of Jimmy Gardner, once an usher on the show who maintained many friendships after he left to go into business, and sold Merle Evans his new home.

Gardner recalls that he often carried Frieda in his arms to the cook house and had a deep admiration for the smiling, plucky girl. Miss Pushnik retired and now lives in California but their close friendship has continued.

The Doll family---Harry, Daisy, Tiny, and Gracie---was billed as "The world's most famous midget entertainers" and trouped with circuses for nearly half a century.

"They were with me on the 101 Wild West Show," Merle recalls.

"The Doll family was prominent in the side show for many years before they retired; all of them were good friends of mine and very good troupers.

"We had only four of those long-necked women from Burma and they were small; tiny I'd say. Their necks were stretched I'd say twelve to fourteen inches and they wore brass rings from their shoulders to their chins.

"Roland Butler really did a build-up job on them. He got some solder wire and wound it around big wooden spools. Then he took pictures and superimposed the women's heads on these spools; made 'em look sensational, with necks like camels.

"Sometimes people would claim the women's necks didn't seem as long as they looked in Roland's pictures, but they paid to see 'em. They were an excellent attraction as long as they were with us.

"Butler called these gentle little creatures 'giraffe necked women.' He said the long necks were the result of the national sport of 'necking' in Burma.

"According to Butler, these were maidens who had roamed the jungles in Burma, looking for men, and the rings were to keep the men from choking them. He billed them as 'the last of the unknown peoples of this earth;' said they were 'a thousand years behind our epoch,' and a few other such things. That gives you an idea of how Roland worked. He was one of the best.

"After a couple of years on the show, the women went back to Burma. When they left, they promised Butler they'd quit chasing men. We had a big laugh over that."

But one of the biggest drawing cards the circus ever had was the Ubangis. These truly strange people took a liking to the show's head noise-maker and looked upon him as the ruling spirit of the performance.

"These eight women with the saucer lips were the best attraction we had in the 1930s," Merle recalls. "I'd say they were the greatest single attraction I ever saw. I believe Howard Bary brought them in. He brought over a lot of attractions for us in those days.

"Roland Butler named them 'Ubangis' and called them 'The world's most weird living humans---New to the civilized world.' I think he got the name from a river down in Central Africa. I'm not sure that's where they came from but it probably is.

"Anyway, the bills said they were 'Monster-mouthed Ubangi savages with mouths and lips large as full-grown crocodiles; from Africa's darkest depths! ' He painted the lips for posters and they looked the size of turkey platters. They were big, all right; but not that big. They were more like good-sized saucers or bread plates.

"The first year we had these Ubangis, we opened at the Coliseum and moved into the Garden later. I heard they cost the show $1,500 a week and it sounds reasonable. They ranged from sixteen to about forty-five years of age and were worth every penny they cost.

"They brought these Ubangis up from the ship in a rubberneck bus and I've often wondered what they thought riding up Fifth Avenue in New York; seeing all the skyscrapers, neon lights, and a lot of other things they'd never seen before.

"When they first came to this country, they were put in one big room with shower baths, flush toilets and such things. It was the first time they'd ever seen flush toilets and when they were flushed, these women would get scared to death and try to run away.

"But the showers were different. When they'd put 'em in the shower bath and turn on the water, boy! Did they ever love that! They couldn't get enough shower baths.

"They wore garments like big towels wrapped around the waist. And they all went barefooted. So Jeanie Carson, head of the wardrobe department, took them downtown in New York and had clothes put on 'em. They put on short skirts and turtle-neck sweaters, and had shawls around their shoulders. They even put shoes on them; they'd never worn shoes or much of anything else.

"So we put them in this room and fixed it up with tables, ice box, stove and beds. But when we made our first jump, from New York to Boston, they didn't like the accommodations in this railroad car. They beefed something terrible. So we took out all the beds and let 'em sleep on the floor. That satisfied them.

"We took 'em from the train to the circus in a special bus. They had their own tent on the lot and stayed there, with two men from the Burns Detective Agency guarding it.

"When they'd bring food in to them, they'd put the meat and fish and all the food in buckets and eat out of them. The show patrons weren't allowed to get near them---the Burns men would keep them at a distance. So the people would just stand off and gawk.

"There was a stage in the menagerie tent where they'd show off these Ubangis. One ticket would admit you to the main show and the menagerie; so you could see the performance, the menagerie, and the Ubangis.

"They had these three musicians---at least they called 'em musicians. Two played bongo drums and the other had a xylophone strapped to his neck. I remember it had calabash resonators. I don't know how he came to have this xylophone.

"About halfway through the performance we'd parade these Ubangi women around the hippodrome with those three musicians leading the way. Then would come a priest, and then the old chief, Chief Neard. After him came the Chief's wife, Princess Aimidan; then his three lesser wives and the other saucer-lipped women—eight in all.

"Bringing up the rear would be Dr. Bergonnier—Dr. Ludwig Bergonnier, their manager, and his wife. This Dr. Bergonnier was a Frenchman who'd been with them some time; brought 'em out of Africa, I think. But they didn't trust the doctor much.

"The show announcer was the lecturer and we'd stop the show so he could tell about these saucer-lipped women. Oh, they were a big attraction; excellent attraction.

"The only trouble was, we couldn't keep clothes on 'em. All of them were substantially built, especially in the chest, stomach and hips. And they liked to go bare to the waist. We were lucky to get 'em to wear shawls.

"And they'd eat anything—beef, fish, chicken, pork, bananas, oranges, and anything else from the cookhouse. They liked boiled beef and fish, oranges, and bananas. I guess that's what they ate in their native land.

"This Dr. Bergonnier was their sponsor and business manager but they sure didn't trust him. Later they began to suspect he was making a fortune off them and despised him. The old chief had a big wooden chest where he kept their money. He wouldn't let it out of his sight, day or night.

"The women took to carrying miniature figures of Dr. Bergonnier and they'd torture these in mysterious ways, pinching 'em and sticking them with pins. Their hate and antagonism for the doctor mounted until he had to leave the train—couldn't even travel with them. So he left and went to Sarasota.

"He died there the very day the show got into winter quarters. The Ubangis heard he was dead but they wouldn't believe it. So old Chief Neard and the three musicians went to the funeral home to see for themselves. They wanted to make sure he was dead, so they went in and lifted up his eyelids to check. Then they were satisfied.

"They loved soda pop; strawberry was their favorite flavor. And all of them had two teeth out up here and two down below, to fit the great long stems of pipes they smoked. These pipes had stems a foot long or more. All of them slept a lot, too, right on the floor—they didn't like beds.

"Some claimed they'd take these big wooden disks out of their lips at night, but I never saw 'em out. As far as I know, they kept 'em in all the time. They'd put the wooden disks in when they were young, to start stretching the lower lip. According to Dr. Bergonnier, the bigger the lip the more gorgeous the girl.

"Once when I was doing vaudeville in Philadelphia, we played for the masked ball and they had these Ubangis there as a special added attraction. I had sixty musicians in my orchestra, and to make it circusy we put on red coats and were down in the orchestra pit.

"Oh, it was a big place; seating five thousand people. And it was a full house. We had these Ubangis on stage and the guy gave a lecture on 'em. At a certain signal, I was to push a button to bring the orchestra up out of the pit.

"When I pressed the button, up came the orchestra---slow, slow but rising right up out of the woodwork. When the Ubangis saw all these red coats coming up, they broke out of there and took off down an alley. Christ, did they take off! Ran like a bunch of scared rabbits.

"The whole place was in an uproar. Nobody knew what they'd do, and we had one hell of a time rounding 'em up.

"The old lady, the one about forty-five with the biggest lips, she liked me. She gave me a card with the words, 'I love you' scrawled on it like a child wrote it. I still have it among my souvenirs. And she gave me a ring she'd made out of some sort of stiff wire twisted into a circle. I've still got that, too.

"The last time I saw them it was funny. They left the Seaboard station in Sarasota to go home. Dr. Bergonnier was dead and they'd been with us two years, so we sent them in a railroad car to New York on their way home to Africa. I hear they started a very successful ranch with the money they made over here.

"The car they traveled in was a combination chair car and baggage car. Well, they stocked it with soda pop and bananas, apples and oranges---all this fruit for them to eat on the trip north.

"Several of us from the show went down to see 'em off---Carl Hathaway, Con Colleano, George Smith, myself, and several others. George Smith had a quart of whiskey and he went around offering each one of 'em a drink.

"They'd hold their hands under the lips and George would pour the whiskey on the lips. Then they'd tilt 'em up and drink, like drinking coffee from a saucer.

"This old lady, she kept inching closer to me, wanted to kiss me goodbye! Ugh---I settled for a quick handshake."

14

Band Leader and the Animals

Wild animals have been an integral part of the circus since the Pharoahs kept lions as pets, Dionysius trained ferocious beasts, and spectacles were presented in the Colosseum in Rome.

Merger of the Ringling Bros. and Barnum & Bailey circuses introduced the largest traveling menagerie this country had ever seen, including many rare species and everything in the animal line from aardvarks to Zebras.

"Patrons are afforded more than an hour's time before the performance begins to leisurely inspect the mammoth menagerie of rare animals, many of them never before seen in America," said the program.

The menagerie tent was always near the Big Top, and a ticket to the performance also was good for admission to the menagerie. Keepers usually did a masterful job of controlling their beasts, but the whinny of a horse or growl of a tiger comes on like a human sneeze and there's no known method of prevention.

Thus many a time during the concert or main performance Merle Evans and his musicians had to compete with the throaty roar of a lion, the chatter of monkeys, and the screech of birds, together or separately.

The program included everything from white doves, pigeons and canaries to dogs, bears and elephants. Some of these never posed any problems but others did. It was a natural occupational hazard for the musicians, one they had to be ready for and to cope with.

There would be times when doves, apparently confused by the lights and noise, would flutter about the ceiling of the Big Top, defying the band to bring them down. The human statue in the center ring would sway just a bit anxiously and the band director, fully aware of what was going on, signalled for soft music. After all, the band was the only thing on the circus to deal with the situation.

The music would grow softer and softer, almost to a whisper while the crowd waited breathless and unmoving. Finally the birds would drop into place, one by one, as if guided by some unseen hand. The band would break quickly into a smear, the audience would respond with thunderous applause, and the ringmaster would whistle the next act into the ring.

Not only must the band keep attuned to the animals in the ring or overhead so the act would be presented most effectively and without a hitch, but it must be ready for any emergency. No one could predict when a horse might fall and fail to clear the burning barrier. Nor when an elephant would refuse to step lightly on a pretty girl's head, and instead would stand on hind legs to perform a graceful pirouette.

After all, who but his keeper can talk to an elephant? And when lions and tigers are snarling and slinking around the center ring, tempers flare and smothered hates break into the open, as happened one night while Merle and his band played "Jungle Queen" to signal the end of the wild animal act and to bring on the clowns.

"Lion fight! " a man screamed, and the crowd was chilled to numbness by the savage roars.

"Repeat to the double bar and play to the hog-eye," Merle Evans shouted over his shoulder.

The lions had just gone into the runway leading from the ring. Fritz Olson, the trainer, had turned his back to unfasten the latch on the runway door. He tried to seize a lion by the tail and drag him back into the ring when Bottong, biggest beast in the act, crouched, roared, quivered, and sprang. A moment later his jaws were clamped on Olson's arm.

"Stars and Stripes Forever! " Merle Evans yelled, lifting his stubby little cornet to his lips and giving out a sharp, stabbing tone. The band took it up and the crowd sat petrified with fright.

Helpers armed with iron pikes and clubs separated the fighting beasts while Bottong went to his pedestal at the urging of Olson and his whip. Then the lions, one by one, sneaked out through the runway gate, tails between their legs. The crowd broke into applause like thunder and the band broke into "It's a Hap, Hap, Happy Day," to bring in the clowns.

"I remember one time the Ringlings brought over a big sea elephant from Hagenbeck's Zoo in Germany," Merle recalled. "They showed it in Madison Square Garden with six horses pulling the wagon while the announcer did his stuff.

"This creature's name was Goliath and he got special treatment, of course. He had a 70-foot car on the train, with sand at one end and water at the other. After they sent the thing to Sarasota for the winter they put him on the beach at St. Armand's Key.

"Roland Butler, the press agent and master of his craft, wrote billing matter for him saying Goliath was the biggest thing ever to hit the circus. He told the press Goliath was eating 490 pounds of fish a week and growing at the rate of half a ton a year.

"Goliath was what science calls a dugong or sea cow. He was attacked by an octopus or something like that while he was over on St. Armand's Key. When they brought him to winter quarters to get ready for the tour, he was a sorry looking creature.

"Roland and Mr. John worried about Goliath. They thought he wouldn't live to make the tour, so they called in experts. But he got worse and soon passed away. I heard he cost the show $30,000."

Merle also remembers the pygmy elephants as "a good drawing card, but they only lasted two or three years."

Howard Bary also brought them in, and Butler did a masterful job, picturing the gentle little beasts with bodies the size of Shetland ponies and ears almost touching the ground.

"The first and only family of pygmy elephants ever to set foot on this continent," the program read. "Direct from Africa's darkest depths. Not babies but full-grown tuskers, brought to this country after three years of intensive jungle exploration...at a staggering financial outlay."

As a young reporter covering circus doings for the Sarasota *Daily Tribune,* the writer later asked Butler what ever happened to the pygmy elephants.

"The damn things grew up! " he roared.

Merle and his band played for the most temperamental horse, obstreperous tiger, or forgetful elephant, so the missing portion of the act went unnoticed by the crowd. But he could never abide the seals, whom he considers pampered imposters.

"Seals are tone deaf," he says. "They have no earthly idea what the hell they're doing. They obey orders from the keeper.

"Oh, they'll toot what the handler calls 'My Country 'tis of Thee,' but it's terrible; ugh! Sounds something like a baby trying to say its first words, off-key. There's no rhyme nor reason to it. They just blow those damned horns for fish, that's all. I wouldn't have 'em around, if it was left to me. They're the biggest frauds on the show."

Merle's dislike for seals may go deeper than that. Roland Butler once said he caught Evans and his friend, Fred Bradna, taking fish from the seal pens to make snacks for themselves. However, that just may have been one of Butler's bon mots. He had a storehouse of them.

The one animal that tried Merle's soul was a white miniature spitz, a bitchy little thing named "Nelly Kelly" with tail curled over her back. The dog joined Ella Bradna's "Act Beautiful" in Cleveland the first season she used twelve dogs.

A woman who said she could no longer provide a good home for her pet presented Nelly Kelly to Ella and it soon became a favorite of the Bradna couple. Ella lost no time putting her into the act.

Nelly Kelly took an immediate dislike to the band leader and would lie in wait for him. This likely grew out of the band leader's practice of letting go with a fearsome wail on his cornet in the back yard to let performers know it was time to don costumes and makeup, much like a bugler calling the horses to post.

At the first blast of the horn, Nelly Kelly would dash out from beneath a wagon or behind a pile of canvas to rush at Merle with a series of piercing yaps, baring her teeth and snapping at trousers, ankles, or shoes. If Merle aimed a swift kick, the barking increased both in tempo and volume.

When Ella Bradna's dog act came on, Nelly Kelly would make at least one sweep past the band stand for a final assault on the leader before going on stage in the center ring. Merle tried to always keep an eye on the beast and be ready with a well-aimed kick.

Nelly Kelly trouped for six or seven years and never let up. When she died mysteriously, Bradna claimed she had been poisoned and strongly hinted Merle might have been responsible. To this day Merle swears he had nothing to do with Nelly Kelly's demise, but fellow troupers recall he was the only one around who never shed a tear for her.

"Why should I?" Merle asks in all sincerity. "She was nothing but a pesky little bitch. Even her owner gave the dog away, didn't she?"

Merle and his wife have owned two dogs and now are as much in love with their neighbor's pet as they were their own. One of the Evans' dogs was a lovable black Pekingese named "Mr. Boots," born on a circus train in upstate New York, and a trouper to the very end. He lived to the ripe old age of fourteen.

Merle did all he could to prolong Mr. Boots' life, taking the dog on many visits to Dr. John Scully, for many years the circus veterinarian who later went into business in Sarasota.

"I used to take Mr. Boots up to his place on the road to winter quarters," Merle recalls. "Took him there many times. This Scully was quite a doctor and had a good practice; treated all kinds of animals but mostly dogs after he left the show.

"This last time Mr. Boots was really sick and nothing seemed to do him any good. So after we'd tried everything else—all kinds of pills and injections—Doc Scully says to me, 'Give the dog peanut oil baths.' I was to give him a bath everyday in this peanut oil, you see? And they cost five dollars apiece.

"Well, after I'd tried 'em six days in a row, I could see they weren't doing Mr. Boots any good, so I stopped that. He finally passed away and we never knew from what. Whoo-ee. Five dollars a day, just to give the dog a bath! "

15

Trouping in Foreign Lands

Merle Evans quickly established his reputation as the outstanding cornet player and circus band leader in America. With the prestige of the Ringling Bros. and Barnum & Bailey Combined Shows, plus his years of experience in the entertainment world, he had but to perform with his usual verve and enthusiasm to assure continuous employment.

All he needed to do was pass the word that he was available for work when the circus was in winter quarters, and offers poured in. One of these came from Bertram Mills, a prominent circus operator at Olympia in London, and it happened this way:

John Ringling, who made frequent trips abroad to find new circus acts, buy art, and visit the casinos and spas, became a good friend of Mills, the son of a London coach builder.

The Englishman had visited America when he was eighteen years old and developed an interest in circuses. He also liked the American show wagon, a light, four-wheeled vehicle widely used on horse shows.

Back home in London Mills introduced the coach from his father's factory and it became known as the Mills wagon. When World War I intervened and the government took over his coach-building business, Mills was assigned the task of buying feed for horses in the British Army.

After the war, coach building declined rapidly as automobile production went up, and Mills was unsure where to turn his energies at the moment. He attended a circus at Olympia during the Christmas season of 1919 and was asked what he thought of it.

"If I couldn't put on a better circus than this," he replied scornfully, "I'll eat my hat." This got him a wager of one hundred pounds.

The Ringling Bros. and Barnum & Bailey Circus was the biggest and best Mills had ever seen, and he made up his mind to bring the entire show to Olympia the following season. That would win his wager hands down.

But transporting a circus of this magnitude across the Atlantic Ocean was an impossible dream, or at least much too expensive. So Mills decided he'd do the next best thing. He hired agents and set out to visit as many circuses and book as many outstanding acts as he could.

He sent a cablegram to his friend John Ringling. It read: "I want that band leader of yours. Want Lillian Leitzel and some of your other first-rate acts."

Mills assembled a vast array of acts and attractions, then attempted to blend them into a compact circus. It was a tougher job than combining the Ringling and Barnum circuses, in limited time. Mills had such a collection it took days to get it into shape. He cut and trimmed but it still seemed impossible to put on a creditable performance. At last he had reduced the assemblage to where he was ready for dress rehearsal. That lasted more than four hours. Mills and his equestrian director stayed up all night after that, cutting here and there. They came up with a show lasting for two and one-half hours.

When the Bertram Mills Christmas Fair opened in mid-December, 1920, for a six weeks run, there stood Merle Evans, resplendant in gold-braided uniform, with a band of twenty-eight pieces representing the best musicians from the Coldstream, Welsh, Irish and Grenadier Guards.

"I had a good band, an excellent band," Merle remembers. "Had the best musicians in the British Isles---a fine band."

Lillian Leitzel performed her incredibly beautiful and thrilling act. The Siegrist-Silbon aerial troupe featured Charlie Siegrist and Eddie Silbon. Several other acts and half a dozen of the leading clowns from the Ringling-Barnum Circus made the Mills show a resounding success.

"We had a very good band and Bertram Mills had an excellent show, excellent show," Merle says. "We stayed eight weeks that first season, in December and January, and business was terrific. Mills made good on his promise to put on an excellent circus.

"We entertained the Duke of Windsor, who at that time was Prince of Wales and later became King of England. We had a lot of Lords and Earls---that sort of thing. Every time we'd have ths 'spec' and pass the royal box, I'd let out a little bit on my cornet---damn near blow 'em out of the box. I had a good time.

"Mills featured such things as polar bears, elephants, liberty horses, and great riding acts along with outstanding aerialists. His circus went under canvas in 1930 and was highly successful. After his death in 1938, his sons, Cyril and Bernard, carried on."

Merle made four trips to London to lead the band on the Mills Circus, and became sea-sick as soon as the ship passed the Statue of Liberty.

"Oh, was I ever sea-sick!" he recalls. "Every trip I got sea-sick; thought I would die. But we had a good time in London. No theaters were open on Sunday in those days, but I'd go to band concerts and go sightseeing---to the Tower of London, watch the changing of the guards; that sort of thing.

"Bertram Mills had a country place and we'd go out there some weekends, if the weather wasn't too bad. Oh, the weather was lousy, but the food was good. I really enjoyed my trips to London with the Mills Circus."

Romance also entered Merle's life in London, for there he met Margaret Mills, an English girl who was a dancer and aerialist on the Ringling-Barnum show. Margaret lived near London and went home each winter. So when Merle Evans, Lillian Leitzel, and others from the circus went to London, Margaret dropped in to see them.

"I never spoke to her before I saw her in London," Merle explains. "On the circus, you dare not speak to a girl. The Ringlings had a strict set of rules about fraternizing. You were not allowed to speak to the ballet girls. They'd fine you for it.

"Any chance meeting with one of the show girls in the park or in the city was inexcusable. I remember the Ringlings even fired a manager once, for breaking the rules. All the single girls slept in what we called the 'virgin car' and it was off-limits for any male. All the girls were chaperoned and guarded.

"I started going out with Margaret in London, so when we went back on the Ringling show, I told Mr. Charlie I was going to marry her. He says, 'All right,' so we were married in 1926."

On his last trip to London in 1924, Merle met the members of a Czechoslovakian band then en route to America. Sam Gumpertz, who had promoted many entertainment ventures in his busy career including Eugene Sandow, the strong man, and Harry Houdini, the magician, was bringing the Czech band to America to play at Coney Island.

"Later, Gumpertz got a bright idea," Merle relates. "He sold his friend, John Ringling, on bringing the band to Florida to play. Mr. Ringling was promoting real estate and band music was a good thing to draw a crowd.

"It was a big band of about thirty players and they had real snappy uniforms---dark green with a lot of brass buttons, as I recall. They didn't get much money---I think twenty dollars a week and a place to stay, which wasn't much in those boom times.

"They lived in an old shack back of the John Ringling Hotel, a construction shack left there. They slept and cooked their meals there; rehearsed and did everything right out back of the hotel. Tourists could see them from the windows or on their way to the beach.

"They could play those European marches and they had some instrumentations. They had C-tubas and E-flat tubas and all that stuff. It was an excellent band but they couldn't play in town---the union wouldn't stand for it.

"They played in Pershing Square over on St. Armand's Key where John Ringling had his big real estate promotion. Their music was different from ours but it was good. I remember one time they took this Czech band to Tampa. It was for Gasparilla or some such civic activity. But the union stepped in and they didn't play a note.

"Then the real estate boom busted and the band broke up. Some went home but others stayed. I had one with me for years---he was a good baritone, named John Horak."

Merle's next tour took him to Cuba in the late 1940s and early 1950s when the circus visited Havana after the U.S. season ended. The band leader had some interesting and amusing experiences there, due primarily to his inability to speak Spanish. He knows only English and circus-ese.

Under Cuban law, the circus could use only Cuban musicians and Merle found few of them understood English although music is the universal language. He solved the problem by having band instructions printed on large cardboard placards. Merle would flash these for cue and tempo changes and did it with such speed and dexterity that Havana newspapers reported he was the only band leader in the world who also was a juggler and performed while leading the band.

His musicians represented a vivid cross section of Havana males ranging from taxi drivers and policemen to university professors and clothing merchants. It was not unusual to have a player miss the performance on account of his university classes or a police sergeant drop his horn to arrest a miscreant in the crowd.

The circus' Havana stands, with props and animals going by steamer from Tampa and performers by air from Miami, were a tremendous financial success. However, they ended on a sad note for Merle, whose wife Margaret picked up an amoebic infection on the 1950 tour.

"When we got back and went to New York," he says, "they started giving her a lot of shots and pills, but her heart just couldn't take it. She passed away in a New York hospital."

The band leader's next extended visit out of the country came in 1961 when the circus sent a unit to Rio de Janeiro for a South American tour which lasted three months.

Performers included the Cristianis, a versatile family of seven bareback riders, trapeze artists, tumblers, and balancers who once operated their own circus. Also on the tour was Unus, "the man who stands on his forefinger," and several other leading attractions.

Arthur M. Concello, who had graduated from the flying trapeze to become general manager of the circus for his friend, John Ringling North, arranged Merle's next trip abroad, which became a combined business and pleasure jaunt.

By now Merle had married Nena Thomas, a sprightly red-head who also has deep roots in the circus. A native Texan, Nena was married to Harry Thomas, equestrian director of the Tim McCoy Circus. They then moved to the Cole Bros. show in 1941, where Nena did a riding act.

"They gave me a mare and all the other horses in the act were stallions," she recalls. "The minute I got in the ring there was loud neighing and these stallions would come charging at us. The mare had the good sense to bolt and get away from there. I usually ended up on the ground."

Nena divorced Thomas in 1950 and met Merle Evans soon afterwards when both hitched a ride with a mutual friend. Two years later they were married, and Nena went to work in the circus office.

"Now about the European trip," Merle recalls. "We were playing Chicago at the time. Concello comes to me and he says, 'You need a vacation. Get away from here for a while. I'm sending you and Nena to Europe.'

"I says, 'What about the show?' and he said, 'Oh, don't worry about the show.' So I left Ray Floyd, my assistant who was a very good drummer, in charge of the band, and we took off for Paris.

"It was the latter part of July and they sent about sixty people over there. They put in a three-ring show and it was excellent, but the Europeans were used to one-ring circuses and never did take too well to three rings.

"I took the music over there and broke in a Dutch band leader. We opened in Lille, France, and stayed there a week. I did the first three weeks of the tour and Concello, who was with us, said to me, 'You need to get away from here.' I says, 'What about the show?'

"He said, 'Oh, don't worry about the show.' So we went sightseeing in Paris, then went to Madrid, Rome, Zurich---we went all over and had a wonderful time. I think Spain is my favorite country outside the United States.

"I asked Art when he wanted me back on the show and he says, 'Oh, don't worry about the show. Enjoy yourselves.' So we went back to New York---had an apartment in Belvedere Hotel. We stayed there and saw the Philharmonic and some shows, and we saw the World Series! Then I went back with the circus to finish out the season."

Merle had another interesting and educational trip abroad, to Russia in 1963. Again it was Concello who arranged to send a circus unit to Moscow, through the U.S. State Department's cultural exchange program. The circus had lost a million on its first European venture and half a million on the World's Fair in New York, but Concello was still in command and going strong.

"I took along my music and spent two weeks there," Merle says. "I rehearsed the band and then turned it over to a Russian leader. I had a girl interpreter, a lady of about twenty-five, and she was excellent. She was the same translator Leonard Bernstein used with the New York Philharmonic. She spoke very good English.

"One of the acts wanted a waltz and I looked it over and it didn't sound good to me. But they wanted it so we played it. After the first show, they came to me and said they didn't like it themselves. So they told me 'Play what you like.' I dropped that Russian waltz and played 'Sunnyland' instead. They liked that.

"They wanted to use a lot of violins. Now, violins are never used on circuses in this country, or in other parts of Europe or South America. But these Russians wanted 'em so I took my score and made a fiddle book out of it.

"The first day, we had a violin in rehearsal; next day they had two, then four. We wound up with ten violins! I had never heard of ten fiddles in a circus band.

"We had three trombones, five cornets, some basses and a piano. The Russians are excellent on the strings and good pianists. We had fourteen women in the band, which was really an orchestra playing band music. We had excellent string and piano players; good trumpets and saxophones, too.

"So it turned out to be strictly orchestra, playing circus music. They weren't used to our quick changes but they soon got into it; turned into an excellent band.

"They had girls operating the spotlights; had a wonderful lighting system and the finest subway system in the world. They had eighty circuses in Russia; thirty of them played only in buildings---one ring shows.

"I'd say their bear acts were the greatest I ever saw. And they had a lot of jugglers, trapeze acts, wire walkers, and performers on the bars. And they had excellent clown acts. We went to a graduation of the Russian School for Clowns. It was a very fine school for all circus performers, something we've never had in this country.

"We never got out of Moscow, but they took us sightseeing nearly every day. We went to the ballet and shows. The theater where we saw the Bolshoi Ballet was beautiful, with about 120 in the orchestra.

"I wish we could have seen some of Russia outside of Moscow, but they wouldn't let us go outside the city. It was in the summer, July and August, and the weather was nice, but the food was terrible. I was glad to get home."

16

Ringling, Gumpertz and Petrillo

Merle Evans worked for three of the toughest and most explosive characters in show business. That he managed to please or at least pacify all of them is a tribute to his diplomacy and patience. The men, often at loggerheads, were John Ringling, Samuel W. Gumpertz, and James C. Petrillo.

"I'd have to say John Ringling made a big mistake in 1929 when he over-reached and bought the American Circus Corporation for two million dollars. Three smart showmen, Jerry Mugivan, Ed Ballard, and Bert Bowers, organized this outfit in 1921. It operated the Hagenbeck-Wallace, Sells-Floto, John Robinson, Sparks, and Yankee Robinson circuses, or held those titles." Merle recalls.

"They leased Madison Square Garden and decided to put a combination of Sells-Floto and Hagenbeck-Wallace shows in there to open the 1930 season. Well, John Ringling had helped build The Garden, was board chairman at one time, and wouldn't stand for that. He'd always opened in the Garden and thought he always would, but Mugivan, Ballard, and Bowers beat him to it, signed contracts and were all set to take over the spot.

"So Mr. Ringling bought the American Circus Corporation. This gave him control of just about all the important circuses in the country. He showed 'em he was a big dealer.

"If the stock market crash hadn't come along about a month after Mr. John made his big move, he'd have been all right. But after the crash came the depression and he was really in trouble. Business was shot. The depression hung on and Mr. Ringling lost control of the show.

"New York bondholders took it over. That's when Sam Gumpertz moved into the picture. They incorporated in Delaware and Gumpertz went in as senior vice president and general manager. He was the boss, you see. John Ringling still had his name on the program as president but he was on salary---I heard it was only $25,000 a year---and didn't have any voice in management. He was out in the cold.

"Gumpertz was an experienced showman; had promoted a lot of things. And he'd been a close friend of John for years. But when he became boss, they fell out and their friendship froze up. They soon got to hate each other; wouldn't even speak to one another.

"Mr. Ringling was jealous of Gumpertz, I think, and felt he should have some say-so in running the show. After all, it bore his name and he had the title of president, but Gumpertz was boss. It was his job to keep the corporation happy, keep the show going, and make money if he could.

"That wasn't easy in those depression years---1932, '33 and '34. It was rough on everybody. Gumpertz once testified he was forced to borrow $200,000 from Mrs. Edith to put the show in winter quarters. I can believe that.

"Another big scramble for control started right after Mr. John passed away on December 2, 1936. It was just one day short of ten years after Mr. Charlie died. The circus heirs and the corporation battled over the spoils.

"John Ringling North, a nephew of the Ringling brothers, was the winner. North's mother was their only sister, Ida. He had some excellent connections and proved to be a smart financier. He was a good showman, too. They called him 'Young Johnny North'---I believe he was about thirty-four at the time.

"He'd been around the show and worked on it, mostly as a flunky for his old Uncle John. I've still got a picture of Johnny at a cash register out front in 1919. It was a candy stand and he was learning about the circus and finances. After Johnny and his younger brother, Henry Ringling North, raised some money they won over most of the directors and stockholders. That means Sam Gumpertz is out.

"Gumpertz had signed a union contract good for five years from May, 1937. It doubled the pay of workingmen from thirty dollars a month and keep, lower in winter quarters. North wanted to keep the lower scale through New York and Boston, until the show moved under canvas. This had been done before, but union leaders wouldn't have any of it now.

"The strike lasted through the first performance in the Garden and two more. Then it was settled for the remainder of the New York dates and the Boston dates. But we had a lot of labor trouble all that spring and the show finally had to close in Scranton, Pennsylvania, the 22nd of June.

"North was promoting Gargantua and had hired Charles LeMaire, a Broadway showman, to stage a pageant featuring Frank (Bring 'Em Back Alive) Buck. Even my band had Bengal Lancer uniforms.

"North made a wise move when he put Arthur M. Concello in as general manager. Art had been a star of the flying trapeze and was about the smartest showman around; still is, although he is out of it now.

"So what did they do? Sent some of the biggest attractions to the Al G. Barnes---Sells-Floto unit, which was part of the combine. The rest of the show went to winter quarters in Sarasota. We finished out the season and North said we actually showed a profit.

"With the Norths and Concello in command and Gargantua a big attraction, we got through the 1939 season without any serious labor trouble. It was the same in 1940, but when we went to open in 1941, with the war on, we really got it. James C. Petrillo and his union musicians struck the show.

"That really had me on the spot because I had to deal with him, or rather Johnny North did. You see, I was caught right in the middle, between my friends the Norths and Concello, and Petrillo. I'd been a union member since about 1910 and had a lot of friends on both sides.

"This Petrillo can be a very demanding person. Oh, he was a tough one. So was Johnny North. They got into some very hot arguments. I really feel the union was to blame in this case. In the first place, they should have made the contracts in January and not waited until July. North tried to bluff, but you couldn't bluff Petrillo. No sir, nobody could bluff Jimmy Petrillo.

"The union wanted a raise of two dollars and fifty cents a week. My men were getting, I think, fifty-six a week and the union wanted fifty-nine. They also wanted a fifty-cent or maybe a dollar raise for the side show band.

"When they started talking over these deals---Johnny North and the union---I met with Mr. Petrillo and he says to me, 'Well, if you'll pay the show band two-fifty a week more we'll let the side show band stay where it is for now.'

"Everybody was for this but the union representatives. They had come on the show for the new contract and aimed to get it. So the representative says, 'No; we'll have to have two-fifty a week raise for everybody.' You see, he was out to get a better contract all around, for all musicians.

"So in Philadelphia they pulled the band off the show. That's the year they had this Stravinsky elephant ballet. With all the negotiations going on, the show made some plans of its own. They'd set up tape recorders and taped the whole show---had four tapes of the entire performance.

"So the strike came on and we put up picket lines. Oh, I never walked it. I was there, all right, trying to bargain for my men. But I never carried a sign. I was trying to get the two sides together. I wanted the thing settled.

"Johnny North says to me, he says, 'Merle, why don't you come on back and play?' I says, 'John, I couldn't do that. Why, they'd kick me out of the union and I'd never be able to work again. I just couldn't do it.'

"So they played these records on the show the rest of the season. Frank McClosky played the records. He was the manager and assistant to Concello, the general manager. McCloskey now is half owner of Clyde Beatty-Cole Bros. Circus, with Jerry Collins, the greyhound and horse track man.

"So I left the show and went on the Fitch Bandwagon radio show, National Broadcasting Company, with Graham McNamee doing the announcing. It was the first real big band to go on nationwide radio regularly. We made quite a hit. I thoroughly enjoyed it."

About that time, Robert L. Ripley's "Believe It or Not" syndicated feature carried a sketch of Merle Evans and said the Ringling Bros. Circus band master had "Played 7,790 performances in succession without missing a show in 22 years."

This was all the more unbelievable because circus musicians played seven hours a day six days a week in all kinds of weather from extreme heat to numbing cold, from mid-March to late November.

When he wasn't leading the band, Merle wore a large handkerchief tied around his neck, to catch the rivulets of perspiration and keep his shirt collar clean, or to keep out the cold wind.

"Of course, my men were physically exhausted after each show," he says, "but the thrill and satisfaction of a good performance, prospects of a good meal in the cook house, and a visit with friends in the back yard kept us all going.

"That and knowing you'd entertained millions of adoring and appreciative fans coast to coast; seeing old friends and making new ones in every city and town we played. I guess it all helped keep us well and happy.

"To be a real trouper, you have to like people, like traveling a lot, and be willing to put up with some inconveniences and hardships; learn to live with 'em. That was the way it had been with me all my life.

"So now here comes World War II. The strike was on; things were really in bad shape for me and my band. Some of my boys went to other shows, some went into the service; we sort of scattered. Would you believe I wound up in Abilene, Texas, at Hardin Simmons University!

"Years before, the University of North Carolina had offered me a job but I'd turned it down. Now here I was, heading for Hardin Simmons University. And I'd never made it to high school."

17

To College and Back

"I got the job at Hardin Simmons through my old friend, Gib Sandefer," Merle remembers. "He was athletic director at the university. Gib's father had been president of Hardin Simmons for forty years.

"Gib had wired me and asked me to call him. So I called and he says, 'We'd like to have you come down and take charge of our band. Mr McClure, the band leader, is going into the Army.'

"It's more like a show band than any other in America because they play for football games and rodeos and things like that---it uses a lot of brass and smears, that sort of thing. We played for just about everything and anything that came along.

"So Gib says 'Come on down,' and I says to him, 'I've got no diploma or anything in this school or college business; I'm just a greenhorn. Never got to high school; only eighth grade.' And he says to me, 'That makes no difference. Your experience means more to us than any degree. We know your reputation.'

"So I went out there to Abilene. We had about a forty-piece band. The musicians wore chaps and cowboy boots and the big cowboy hats. I had a pair of fifty-dollar boots, a big cowboy hat and chaps, too---I had the works. Even had a horse to ride. The school had about fifty horses and the one they gave me to ride was one Bing Crosby had used in some pictures he'd made. I used to ride this horse quite a lot.

"The band wasn't mounted; we just had the horses to ride. They had a good football team and I was the biggest 'peppy' around. I'd lead the band and we'd all whoop and holler. We played Texas Tech, Texas Christian, Baylor, and teams like that.

"We'd make the trips to football games in two cattle trucks. We'd put benches in there and load the band for these ball games. The trucks

Merle Evans as director of the Hardin Simmons University band in 1942 with Marion McClure, his predecessor, Sheriff Will Watson, and Gib Sandefer, the athletic director.

weren't covered, but we'd spread canvas over the top. It would really get cold on some of those trips.

"I'd been there a month or maybe six weeks and one day Dean Campbell says to me, 'I don't see you at any of our teachers' meetings,' and I says, 'I didn't know I was supposed to make them.'

"Well, he says, 'Don't you ever look in your box in the office?' I says, 'Why, I look in it a couple of times a month, to see if you put the pay check in.' He seemed a little startled, so I says, 'Next time you have one of these teachers' meetings, let me know. I'd like to come.'

"He called me three or four days later and said there'd be a teachers' meeting, so I got in touch with my friend Gib and we went. I stuck a pencil behind my ear and stuffed some paper in my pocket and I was all set. I was in business.

"I also went to church; used to go two and three times on Sundays. They had this Victory Bible Class in a theater downtown at ten o'clock and we'd go to the Baptist church on campus at noon. Then we'd go to the school cafeteria for lunch.

"After that I'd go home and maybe lie down for an hour or two in our apartment, where my wife and I stayed. I had this .410 gauge shotgun and we'd ride out in the country and shoot jack rabbits. We'd put a tub in the back of the truck and fill it with jack rabbits.

"We had a couple of fellows taking care of the horses and I'd give them a dollar each to clean these jack rabbits. They'd skin 'em and put in some onions, salt and pepper to flavor them. And they'd cook these rabbits and feed all the dogs on campus. We had maybe ten or fifteen dogs roaming around on campus and when you feed one dog you always get a pack. They'd all come around to eat.

"We never ate those jack rabbits. They weren't anything like our Kansas rabbits. But I'll tell you what we did do. Coming back from those rabbit hunts we'd stop and buy watermelons. They raise wonderful watermelons out there—great, big ones. Delicious!

"Gib's wife made the best tamale pies you ever tasted. My wife and I had this apartment about two blocks from where Gib and his wife lived. So they'd call and we'd go over for an hour or two and eat this lovely tamale pie. It was wonderful. And then maybe we'd go to another Baptist church on the other side of town. I tell you, it got so there I could pray right along with the rest of 'em."

Merle's music classes began at 8 o'clock and he would teach trumpets, trombones, or perhaps a section. He held band practice at 2:30 each afternoon. The band also gave concerts and played at revival meetings.

On Sundays, if there was time, the band might go to a nearby Army camp and entertain patients in the hospital. Merle usually took along a girl who sang and played accordion solos, and a man who entertained by spinning a rope.

"We'd put on a little show for the boys and they liked that," Merle recalls. "We went out to this hospital several times.

"They had about 3,000 students at Hardin Simmons in those days. I had the best old time there and I think I did a lot for the school. If I'd been a few years younger, I might have stayed, but I don't think so. I liked a little more action, more entertainment. There really wasn't much excitement there; in fact, it got sort of dull.

"At these teachers' meetings they'd have about ten guys who did nothing but teach Bible. Gib and I would go in early and sit 'way in back and I'd see these guys come in wearing stiff rubber collars and baggy pants—looked like they had a loaf of bread in their pants, you see?

"I'd say to Gib, 'What does that guy do?' and he'd say, 'He's a preacher.' And I'd say, 'What does this guy do?' and he'd say, 'Why, he's a preacher, too.' They got to calling me 'Doctor Evans' and I says to Gib, 'Hell, if I stay around here five years I'm gonna look like these guys and I'm not gonna do it. I'm getting out of here.'"

The circus had weathered the depression and come back strong under the guidance of John Ringling North and Arthur Concello, with an assist from Gargantua the Great. But World War II was on now and movement and manpower were two major problems. North had a bold recommendation which he placed before the directors. He suggested that the circus suspend operations until after the conflict.

James Fraser drawing celebrating Merle Evans's return as circus band director in 1943

Other members of the family refused to go along; they were afraid if the great old circus ever stopped, it would never get going again. They had some encouragement from government officials in Washington and elsewhere, who wanted the circus to boost morale and help sell war bonds. It did both.

Thus in that troubled year of 1943, the stockholders, most of whom belonged to one or another branches of the family, elected Robert E. Ringling, son of Mrs. Charles, as president. The program featured two spectaculars, "Let Freedom Ring" and "Drums of Victory."

When Robert took over, James A. Haley, who had been an accountant and bookkeeper for John Ringling, became vice president and assistant to the president. At that time Haley stood in very well with the Ringlings. In fact, he was courting Aubrey Black Ringling, whose husband, Richard Ringling, had died in an accident in 1931.

"This Haley is an all right guy," Merle says. "He married Aubrey and they traveled with the show. Later he ran the show, and increased the size of it to 109 railroad cars. After Haley sold out and left the show, he was elected to Congress from the Sarasota district and he's been re-elected ever since. I think he's made a good congressman.

"So about this time I got a call from Robert Ringling, who was in

Lauritz Melchior, the famous tenor, tries his hand at directing the circus band in 1944 (above), and tests his lung power on Merle Evans's cornet (below)

Sarasota. The phone for our apartment was out in the hall, so I told him I couldn't talk there but would call him back. I went down to the hotel and put in a call for him at his home.

"The war was on and there were a lot of shortages. The show was having all kinds of problems, especially with manpower and transportation. A lot of performers and workingmen had gone into service, some had just up and quit; things were in a mess.

"Robert says to me, 'We want you back on the show.' So I said, 'All right. I'll come back.' And he told me what they'd pay me. So I went down to Gib Sandefer's office and told him, I says, 'I've got some bad news for you; I'm going back on the show. I'll be leaving in about two weeks.'

"Well, they tried every way to get me to stay at Hardin Simmons. They had a cowgirl band of about fifty pieces and they wanted me to take that over. They wanted to give me the bookstore to run; wanted to make me the postmaster on campus. They offered me all kinds of inducements if I'd stay.

"But being in show business like I'd been all my life and having these professional musicians, when you get to the college level it's just not the same. The band members didn't want to be musicians; they just wanted to get a degree.

"At Hardin Simmons, some wanted to be preachers, of course. Some wanted to be teachers, go into business; they wanted to be a little of everything except musicians. They weren't at all interested in music as a career.

"It had been a good deal for me at the time, an excellent deal; good experience. I had the best time of my life there and I think I did a lot for the school. At least we had a peppy band, a real good band. But I thought it was too tame for a circus band leader and after a year or more, I was ready to go back on the show. I just wasn't a college man.

"This Robert Ringling was an odd duck. He was an operatic singer in Chicago and had some screwy ideas. One time they bought some Bayreuth tubas. They're German-made things with French horn mouthpieces.

"Robert wanted four of them, and the only place we could get 'em was the Metropolitan Opera in New York. So he started working on the deal to get these tubas. The Metropolitan wanted a horse, so we traded them a white horse for those four tubas. We used them on the show for a while but I finally got rid of them. Know what I did with 'em? Sold 'em to a guy in California!

"Robert was a screwball about French horns. We had four of them and four tubas on the band while he was in command. He always wanted a lot of brass in his circus band.

"And could he eat? Christ, he would eat like he was going to the electric chair. That year we had the fire in Hartford, which I'll tell about later, we were all down here to re-group and re-open in the Rubber Bowl at Akron, Ohio. I never saw a guy liked to rehearse as much as Robert Ringling. He wanted to rehearse for hours every day. I think he just wanted to have the band entertain him with circus music.

"When we went up to Akron, we were rehearsing there before the opening and over the loudspeaker he says, 'I want to see Merle Evans; I want to see Merle Evans.'

"I says, 'What the hell does he want now?' So I go over there and he says to me, 'Merle, I want you to have dinner with us after the show tonight.' Well, that was different. And so I says, 'All right, Mr. Ringling.'

"He says, 'I'll wait for you.' So when the show was over, he was waiting with his chauffeur and I could see he was anxious to get at that food. He was real impatient. And I says, 'Let me wash my hands and I'll be right up.'

"Well, we went back to his car on the train and he took off his coat and you never saw a guy eat like he did. He tore into that chicken like he hadn't eaten for a week, or never expected to see food again. I guess Robert was a pretty good match for his uncle John in the grub department.

"But I always got along fine with all the Ringlings—Charles, John, Robert—all of 'em. After I'd come back to the show from Hardin Simmons, I loaned Robert Ringling $12,500 one time to help move the circus into Madison Square Garden.

"Imagine him, a Ringling, borrowing money from a broken down old band leader like me?"

18

The Troubles of Troupers

Merle Evans trouped in every kind of weather in 48 states and much of Canada during his sixty-year career and has vivid recollections of both the good and the bad.

He remembers playing stands in Pennsylvania and West Virginia when strong winds whipped coal dust into dressing tents in clouds, until everyone seemed to be coming on in blackface.

"It would take us days to get the coal dust out of our hair and off our bodies," he says. "And get a shower of that red dust in Montana and Wyoming! It can color everything red as bricks. Get caught in dust from a limestone or chalk mine and everything turns milky white.

"Under these conditions, a shower bath can be mighty welcome. Try taking a bath in a bucket of water! You end up in worse shape than when you started. One bucket per person was the usual ration."

Any circus traveling under canvas must battle all the natural elements such as rain, wind, heat, and cold, but the most feared and costly of all is fire.

Blowdowns can rip expensive canvas, wreck properties, and cost a date; rains can mire wagons and make the lot unplayable overnight; heat and cold can cause discomfort and cut deeply into attendance.

Tornadoes strike with terrifying swiftness and their damage can be awesome. Merle remembers one in Missouri that picked up the Big Top and tossed it away like an empty laundry bag. It also took the bandstand right out from under his players.

Every member of the band was left standing on his feet but Merle quickly switched to another number and the band played on. He isn't certain to this day if they missed one, two or three beats, but he thinks it was only one.

Fatal accidents among circus patrons are extremely rare, although when the circus came to town, residents and especially children flocked to the lot to watch the show unload and set up. Truck and tractor drivers and all workingmen became highly skilled in dodging these curiosity seekers. So did the elephants and draft horses.

Usually it was a performer or workingman who was injured, on the lot or at the trains. When this happened, it was like a tragedy in the family. The hospital car had its share of cases.

Circus folk not only work together closely eight or even ten months of the year but they grow up and live side by side 24 hours out of every day, Sundays included. Thus a camaraderie develops that is seldom found anywhere else in human relations.

When an accident occurred in the arena, Merle Evans and his band quickly switched to another number, the equestrian director whistled in another act, and the show went on with a minimum loss of time or show of emotion.

The injured performer was rushed outside to a doctor, or shoved into an ambulance and sped to the nearest hospital. Fellow troupers would visit him there if possible but the show went on as usual, and when the engagement was over, it moved to another town.

Merle had what he called his "Chicken song" for such things as a flyer taking a spill or a horse bolting. This has never been written down but all the bandsmen knew it and knew its meaning. Merle simply said, "Stand by, boys; take it from the top."

Two big fires hit the circuses long before they combined. One burned the Barnum & Bailey big top in Schenectady, New York, in 1910, and another consumed the Ringling Bros. tent at Sterling, Illinois, in 1912. No one was seriously injured in either blaze but the financial loss was considerable. An even more costly fire destroyed the menagerie tent of the combined circus at Cleveland, Ohio, on August 4, 1942, taking the lives of 39 animals reportedly worth more than $200,000.

Even then the show carried on. In fact, while veterinarians and keepers worked feverishly to save badly-burned animals, using new drugs made available by the military, the performance inside the Big Top went on. Its "spec" that season, ironically, was "Happy Holidays."

Two years later the circus lost virtually everything but its appeal and its reputation. The most tragic and costly date in all circus history was July 6, 1944, and the place was Hartford, Connecticut.

Merle Evans and many another trouper remembers the occasion with profound sorrow. He and several others barely escaped with their lives. Most will never forget the horrifying experience.

More than 25 years later, Merle would rather not talk about it. He is certain every member of the big circus family did all he could under the harrowing circumstances. Many survivors praised the brave band leader and his men, along with most other circus hands from star performers to lowly workingmen.

"I still wake up nights thinking about the Hartford fire," says Howard Scharman, head usher that day who now lives in Florida and is no longer with the show. "I saw the fire when it started, along the seams over the sidewall near the front door. And I heard the band start playing the 'disaster march.'

"It was going toward the peak, burning the guy ropes. I fought my way into the crowd and started shoving people down through the Bibles (sectional stands so called because they fold into compact units for moving). That way they could scramble out under the sidewalls.

"Some were hollering and screaming and some tried to fight me. But I thought it was better to get them out of there with maybe a sprained ankle than have 'em burn to death.

"I don't know how many I got out but I cleared one or two sections before the fire drove me out. The people just panicked. All this time Merle Evans and the band played the 'disaster march' and everybody on the show tried to get as many out as we could. All of us worked to try to save 'em. We never thought of props at a time like this."

Ralph Emerson, in charge of the elephants that day and now living near Hartford, heard the first strains of the music and knew something was wrong. He recalled recently that he quickly gave the command to the 41 pachyderms in his care and they responded immediately.

"Tails, tails!" he cried, and the elephants queued up in the familiar trunk-to-tail formation and marched out of danger. None was harmed, and Emerson's prompt action probably averted a stampede.

John Menser, now retired and living in Miami, remembers the day well. He was a member of the Hartford police department and was in a squad car that afternoon.

"The circus was set up on Barbour Street in the north end," he recalled. "When I got the call, I went right over and when I got there the fire was still burning. Women and children were piled against the steel tunnel set up for the animals to go into and out of the ring.

"There was nothing but smoldering ruins although the fire burned out in ten or fifteen minutes. The whole thing went up in a hurry. We set up a temporary morgue and my brother, William N. Menser, a member of the state police, started to work on identification. He set up an ID office.

"There wasn't any panic then; everything was orderly. We were trying to get people away and get the victims to hospitals. We called in all emergency equipment from all the towns around.

"Our biggest problem was trying to control the traffic and handle the crowd, with everybody coming in, trying to contact wives and children who'd been to the circus, or relatives. It was a mess.

"They finally identified every body except one. We called that 'Little Miss Marker.' It was the body of a little girl and she had only a few burns on her face. Nobody ever identified the body and for years Tommy Barber and Eddie Lowe put flowers on her grave on the anniversary. It was one of my worst experiences as a police officer."

At police meetings later, Menser recalled, when discussions of fires and crowd control came up, "the general consensus was that someone entering the tent flipped a lighted cigarette and it lodged between a piece of hemp rope and the canvas, and that's how it started."

Merle will never forget that tragic Thursday afternoon. Something caused him to look up and he shifted his gaze from Alfred Court's lions, just completing their act. He saw tiny tongues of flame licking their way across the Big Top at the far end from the bandstand.

At the moment he was ready to give the cue to bring on the Wallendas, described in the program as performers who would "shake hands with death at dizzy heights." Without turning, Merle signaled his bandsmen for a quick switch and shouted, "Disaster march! Hit it hard! " The band broke into "Stars and Stripes Forever."

Performers knew instantly something was wrong. While some rushed to clear the arena of dangerous animals or open paths for patrons, others tried to save the crowd that surged toward the exits in angry, disorderly waves.

There were many women and children in the panicky throng, plus three hundred wounded soldiers from a nearby Veterans Hospital, some of them in wheel chairs.

Circus workers and Red Cross attendants wheeled or assisted all the soldiers to safety but many others didn't make it. Merle believes the band repeated "Stars and Stripes Forever" ten or perhaps a dozen times as patrons fought furiously to escape the huge inverted bowl of canvas that became a flaming furnace.

Tongues of fire swept across the ceiling of the vast spread of canvas; quarter poles smoked and burned while the great 62-foot fir center poles flared into giant torches and swung menacingly as fire gnawed at the lines and canvas that held them in place.

"We played Sousa's march and most of the people walked out," Merle says. "A big center pole fell right across the bandstand, but we kept right on playing."

The International Musician, in its issue of August, 1944, carried this account of the band and its heroism:

"Even though the bandstand, at the eastern end from the main entrance, directly opposite the point where the fire started, was ultimately burned to cinders and the electric organ, kettledrums and the platform itself were charred inches deep, the men played on, their faces blackened, their uniforms scorched, until the last of the six great center poles toppled over and the last section of the burning Big Top fell with it.

"The men of the band did not need to be directed to play loudly enough to make the music heard in the farthest reaches of the enclosure. In circus parlance, they 'blasted' it, thus steadying to some degree the milling throng. And they kept on playing until a falling pole actually hit their platform. Then, even as they ran for safety, the drummer continued to beat out the rhythm. Once outside, they reassembled and started up again."

Merle Evans' cornet had been the warning tocsin and it sounded the alarm in time to save most of the 6,789 persons at the show for that matinee performance, but within fifteen minutes the Big Top was a smoking halocaust and 168 persons were dead or dying.

Not a single circus employee or animal was lost that day, a tribute to the smooth operation and utter devotion as a family. It may be noted, however, that some 60 employees were among the 487 persons treated for burns or injuries.

The fire alarmed and shocked the nation, now deeply involved in World War II. There were cries for safety measures and for punishment of those responsible. Six members of the circus staff, most of them executives, were brought to trial on charges of involuntary manslaughter. Five were convicted.

Merle received a citation from the Saints and Sinners, duly signed by Mayor James J. Walker of New York.

The courts allowed claims of $3,946,335 and the circus was thrown into receivership. James A. Haley, in his capacity as executive vice president, had wisely taken out a $500,000 insurance policy against just such an emergency. The circus also had a capital reserve fund of half a million dollars.

This enabled it to leave Hartford but not until nine days after the fire could it get out of town and go to Florida to re-group and recuperate. It reopened in the Rubber Bowl at Akron, Ohio, on August 4 without canvas. Within seven years all claims had been paid out of insurance and earnings.

Haley, elevated to president in 1946 when Robert Ringling became chairman of the board, took the show on the road for the 1947 season

Dexter Fellows Tent
Circus Saints and Sinners Club
of America
To
Merle Evans
And His Circus Band

In acknowledgment of, and in salute to, your heroism. When fire struck the Ringling Brothers, Barnum and Bailey combined shows during the matinee performance of July 6th, 1944, in the City of Hartford, Connecticut, you proved yourself worthy of the highest principles of the circus trouper by acting in a manner above and beyond the call of duty.

The members of Dexter Fellows Tent are proud to pay you this tribute.

New York, July 7, 1944.

President

Saints & Sinners citation of 1944

Evans (standing, center back row) and his band in 1946

aboard 109 railroad cars — the largest circus ever to tour America.

Then John Ringling North, through some clever maneuvering in administering his uncle's estate, got his hands on one-third of the circus. Under terms of the will, much of Ringling's property was to go to the state of Florida. And while Ringling had cut North out of his will, he did not drop him as an executor of the estate, entitled to a good slice for handling it.

So in 1948 North went back in as president and Arthur M. Concello became general manager with Frank McClosky as manager and Willis Lawson assistant.

"After I went back on the show under Robert Ringling in 1943," Merle says, "I should have asked for more money. After he came back, Art Concello says to me one day, 'You could have named your own ticket when Robert Ringling called you and asked you to come back on the show; could have set your own price.'

"Art's a good friend of Nena and me—lives near us and we visit back and forth. Art's a smart man, very smart man. So when he comes back on the show and tells me I could have named my own price with Robert, I says to him, 'Well,' I says, 'now that you're back in charge, why don't you give me a little more money?'

"Not Art Concello. No sir. He made it up to Nena and me by giving us trips around Europe and in a lot of other ways. But Art Concello doesn't give money away, not even to his best friends."

19

Years of Change and Decline

After North and Concello went back in command early in 1948, it appeared that the "good old days" might be here again for the circus and for a time it rode the tide of post-war prosperity.

Officials called that season "spectacular" and predicted that Concello's portable steel grandstand with its folding upholstered seats and dressing rooms beneath would be its "savior."

Turnaway crowds were the rule in Madison Square Garden and full houses greeted the show in Boston, Washington, Philadelphia, and Baltimore. The circus played Connecticut for the first time since the Hartford fire, showing in Bridgeport, Waterbury, Plainville, and New London.

It visited San Francisco for the first time since 1941, showing in the Cow Palace where Roland Butler reported "seven capacity performances." He added:

"From the standpoint of daily remuneration, the Cow Palace engagement was the most profitable ever played during any circus road tour in the history of the world."

That may be stretching it a bit, but the route book for the 1948 season went into ecstacies in these words:

"John Ringling North produced for 1948 the greatest and the finest circus performance ever seen on land or sea. It was and is truly 'the talk of the nation.' His policies were big show, big business, geared for glory and for gold.'

"Arthur M. Concello, with his magic, portable, unfolding, truck-unit, time-saving grandstands; his steel mesh wild animal arenas, his expert management and his swift, sure decisions had Big Bertha so mobile, so streamlined, and so alert she operated like a well-oiled marionette."

The big show band, Merle Evans directing, had twenty-eight men, including the very durable Paul Davis on horn, John Horak on the baritone and Ray Floyd on the snare drums. Arthur A. Wright's side show band had fourteen players.

Conditions changed rapidly after that. By 1951 the route book noted that "while prophets of doom at every turn in the amusement world wailed that road show business is dead forever," the circus made a "phenomenally successful 17,000-mile coast-to-coast tour of the nation, exhibited in 121 cities in 36 different states, made millions happy, and recorded another glorious circus season on the Dial of Time."

Its press agents talked of "fast moving performances" and stressed "audience appeal," at the same time noting that some writers "criticized the general trend toward modernization of the circus."

"When they started unionizing everything, that's when trouble started," says Merle Evans in retrospect. "Nobody wanted to work; you couldn't get help and what you did get was no good. A lot of towns didn't want you. Shopping centers went up on lots we had used for years; these and apartment houses and condominiums took all the places close to town. Parking became a terrific problem.

" "Railroad rates went up. You'd get into town late after long hauls and couldn't get the Big Top up in time for matinees. It might be 4 or 5 o'clock before you could put on a show. A lot of women had children and they'd have to get home and fix dinner for husbands and families.

"You could see it all coming. The show was being squeezed out. We had all these long hauls and railroads couldn't handle us any more. Four trains! Why, they had no place to put us. A lot of them didn't want us.

"You'd be surprised how many trains have been abandoned and tracks pulled up around the country. In Utica, New York, for example, there aren't any side tracks any more. A lot of other cities are the same way; no place to put the show.

"As I said, railroad rates skyrocketed. Of course, the show raised the price of admission—it had to. When I first went on the show admission was fifty cents and fifty cents for a reserved seat. Now it runs as high as five and six dollars; even more in New York. It varies from one stand to the next.

"All our cities have grown up and spread out, shoving the circus further and further from downtown. It was terrible, but I could see it coming. There just weren't any places left to put the show. It had to go indoors.

"I could see the Big Top days were numbered when we were having all this trouble—railroad trouble, lot trouble, help trouble. It all came in bunches. You couldn't get help; nobody wanted to work and everything was going union.

"That's when I decided to get out, in 1955. They brought in Izzy Chevone to lead the band. He wasn't much on circus music and he didn't have the players. Jim Haley once told me it cost the show one hundred thousand dollars a year for the band, but it was worth it. The band was the heart of the show; everything revolved around it. We put life into the performance and tied the whole thing together.

"If you don't have a good band, you might as well close up. Now all the show carries is the drummer and an organist besides the band leader. All the others are pickup musicians, and they're getting mighty hard to find—people to play circus music.

"After the Big Top went down in Pittsburgh on July 16, 1956, Art Concello designed rigging to use in buildings, for the flying acts—that sort of thing. So the show started using buildings for all stands; it had to.

"When you're playing these auditoriums and convention halls, you're under the local union's jurisdiction. They tell you how many musicians you can use in the different cities—New York so many, Chicago so many, Miami so many, Dallas so many, Los Angeles so many; Milwaukee, St. Louis, Atlanta, so many.

"That's the way it is and that was the beginning of the end for the

Merle Evans's band, gaudily uniformed, in 1955

circus band. Now you don't have musicians with you like in the old days. You have to hire these standbys. The Clyde Beatty show only uses seven musicians; King Bros. six, and Polack three. Carson-Barnes has only organ, trumpet and drums. Nearly all the rest of 'em use records—all canned music.

"After I left the show, Johnny North wouldn't let me play some Shrine Circus dates; he claimed these Shrine shows hurt his circus. Well, a lot of things hurt the circus. You could see conditions changing—railroads, help, the whole picture.

"Buildings are the only salvation now, and sometimes you have to take long, expensive jumps between towns. It takes a day to get set up. Why, in the old days we would move in, set up, and have matinees and night shows; even have a parade!

"I used to love to watch 'em load and unload. What an operation that was! We had a whole army of men, with tractors, trucks, horses, and elephants. Everything rolled on schedule. Big as it was, the show got in and out on time.

"Now it travels in just twenty-five cars and even then has to make some long jumps to get places to play in, like from Hampton, Virginia, to Nashville, Tennessee; from Nashville to Oklahoma City, Dallas to Phoenix. These moves take time, and cost like everything. But a lot of time the convention halls aren't available, something else has them booked. So you take long jumps to where you can play.

"In the old days we played every day, six days a week. Maybe like on Sundays, when we didn't play, we'd move from like Johnstown, Pennsylvania, to Wilmington, Delaware, or maybe Denver to Salt Lake City. But the railroads could take you where you wanted to go, and when.

"Now you have to make the building downtown. Some animal acts and performers travel overland by trailers or automobiles. A lot of people have trailers and follow the show. All the rest of the unit goes on 25 cars; the blue unit 25 and the red unit 25. We used to have a hundred for the show.

"But, like Pat Valdo said when the Big Top went down, he says, 'As long as there's a child, a clown, and a horse on earth, there'll always be a circus.' Well, Pat's gone now, but the show will go on. I think there will always be a show, pretty much as it is now, with more clowns, a lot of thrills, animal and high wire acts—that sort of thing.

"But the big bands are gone, the big specs are out; even the old press agents are gone. Now some local guy recruits the musicians, some local guy handles the press. Maybe he knows very little about the circus, and it doesn't get near the space in the papers it used to get.

Arthur M. Concello, star of the flying trapeze and later general manager of the circus

"It's just not like it was in the old days, and never will be again. So many things have changed. I think—and I hope I'm wrong—but I'll bet in time they'll take one of those two Ringling units, the red or the blue, off the road; operate them as just one show.

"Now they're going into all those concessions, selling all kinds of souvenirs; not on the show but franchising them. They even plan to sell phonograph records, toys, games—everything. Mr. Irvin Feld told us in Milwaukee in July they had to make money on the side to keep the circus going. I don't doubt that.

"And I have to agree with him when he says the circus is the only live entertainment left in the country. It's all there is left to compete with sports—and that's big business. All you have left is the circus, and television.

"I'd like to make a suggestion, but they probably won't listen to an old windjammer like me. If they'd bring Art Concello back, he could make money for the show. Art is the smartest circusman in the country today.

"Of course, Art will tell you he sold the old winter quarters for $350,000, cold cash. Nobody but Art Concello could have done that!"

20

Never Play that Again

"One of the main things about music for the circus," says Merle Evans in retirement, "was picking out the right kind for the acts. That's the thing. Some acts knew what they wanted and sometimes I had to tell 'em what would go best; what would put the act across. Then it was up to my band to give 'em the right beat and tempo.

"I've always stuck to circus music as much as possible. Now, with some of the newer acts, we had to change a little. But with most of them, the music didn't make a lot of difference as long as it fit the act and helped put it across, accentuated the action.

"With circus music you want some cornets, some trombones; you need good drummers. You've got to play so everybody can hear, no matter where the seats are. Miss a beat and you foul up an act, throw the timing off.

"Music is the real pulse of the show, the heart of it. We tied the whole performance together with the band. What's been happening lately is they're getting away from a lot of real circus music; so there aren't any circus musicians coming up.

"I listened to a television program of Sousa's music not long ago but I can't say I enjoyed it. Oh, it was good music and the show was well done, but it wasn't circusy. It didn't have the zip, the volume we want on the show.

"Sousa's music isn't circusy at all. The same thing's true with music by the U.S. Marine Corps band, the Army band, the Navy band, the Air Force band. They're concert bands; play standard military marches, not circus music.

"We played some of the classics and some popular music—mixed it up—but not like other bands and orchestras. Circus marches generally used on the show were written by circus musicians, and we had some good ones. They had the feel for it.

"A circus isn't a circus unless it has a band. Cut out the music and what have you got? Certainly not a show. Circus musicians work harder than anybody else on the show. A performer may be on four or five minutes; we're there from start to finish.

"Circus musicians are known among their professional friends as 'windjammers.' That's because they jam wind into cornets, clarinets, trombones, French horns, baritones, Sousaphones or what have you, for six or seven hours a day.

"In the old days city musicians used to poke fun at us 'windjammers' but a lot of them couldn't make the grade or stand the pace. Most city musicians didn't know what circus music was all about. That's when the bands started going down—when they had to pick up city musicians to fill in.

"But looking at it another way, a lot of circus musicians have gone into big city orchestras—fellows like Foots Webster, Charley Randall, Bennie Henton, and Henry Waak. I've never heard of a city-trained musician who could hold down a chair in the old circus band.

"Most circus troupers came from small towns. They'd think and act quickly, didn't have any easy-going traditions to overcome. And if he was a musician, he could play classical stuff as well as the popular music.

"They were tough guys—a healthy, happy lot. I never heard of a case of pneumonia on the show once we left the drafty Madison Square Garden and got under canvas. And we had no typhoid or other such diseases although we changed drinking water every day. Open air kept us healthy, until conditions under the Big Top got better.

"Windjammers once worked for twelve or fourteen dollars a week and got rotten food in the cook house. They slept two in a berth, three berths high, and we had long, tiresome street parades.

"I once played seventy-six full-length marches on top of a seven-ton, stiff-springed wagon in Detroit before both afternoon and evening performances. And I can still remember the mile of cobblestones on the parade route leading to the circus lot in Syracuse, New York.

"Later salaries went up, we slept in first-class Pullmans, one man in each upper berth and two in the lower. We ate at our own table in the best cook house on the road, and they cut out street parades!

"God bless the Ringlings for that, and I say it in reverence. It was tough to ride a bandwagon an hour or more on some hot day in Washington, Cincinnati, or Kansas City. Or in a lot of other cities and towns across the country.

"On a nice spring day, on a fresh, clean lot, life seemed pretty good and it was. But the weather could change overnight, and so could the towns. We had hot weather, cold weather, wet weather, dry weather, windy weather—we had all kinds.

The cornet was his trademark, and he was seldom seen without it

"Sure, we had sore lips now and then. Any lip that vibrates in a cornet mouthpiece or a woodwind reed six or seven hours a day is likely to get sore, especially if the musician has uneven teeth. I had one—Joker Dalzell was his name—played Sousaphone with us, used to file his teeth to make 'em smooth.

"I always was blessed with good teeth all my life, but I had to play with a dry lip, so hot weather was apt to bother me some. Wet weather wasn't so good, either. We often played in rain and mud week after week. But the boys carried raincoats if it looked like rain and there's a trick to keeping dry. It was usually the towners who got wet.

"Of course, no matter what happened, the band had to keep playing—even in a blowdown. I remember once when a storm came up, we played for three-quarters of an hour without stopping. The show couldn't go on, but we had to play. When the storm let up, performers came out of the wagons where they'd taken refuge and the show went on.

"A musician in a circus band has to know his business. If I lifted a finger or nodded my head, it meant something; meant 'Do something and do it quick.' And the stuff we played wasn't easy.

"A man who joined out with me was supposed to be able to play, without rehearsal, overtures from Wagner's 'Tannhäuser' and 'Lohengrin,' Weber's 'Der Freischütz' and 'Oberon,' Beethoven's 'Egmont,' Mendelssohn's 'Ruy Blas,' Verdi's 'Aida,' Saint-Saens' "Samson and Delilah,' Tschaikowski's '1812' and a lot of other standard selections like that. It was all in a day's work.

"In the regular big show program, working on a split-second schedule, they had to snap into stuff by Rossini, Tobani, Schubert and Puccini. We used to open the elephant act with part of a polonaise by Chopin. Then, in the next five minutes, we'd go into a fox trot, a march, two-step, another march, a waltz, a jazz number, and still another march.

"So you can see why the twenty-five or thirty windjammers and drummers in my band had to be alert and watch their cues. We had fifteen stops, starts and changes of tempo in Lillian Leitzel's act alone. Everything had to be timed to the quarter-second.

"And there were half a dozen other numbers just as complicated. That's why a country amateur or a city musician was apt to be over his head when he tackled a circus program. Most of my men came from small town Silver Cornet bands.

"If a small town band practiced six hours a month it's members figured they were doing wonders. My band played six or seven hours a day! Naturally, this would knock the average musician off his seat.

"A fellow came up to me in Zanesville, Ohio, one day and said the best tuba player in the state lived right there in Zanesville. I said I'd like to see him and he told me, 'You're lookin' at him.' He couldn't make the grade with us.

"I always tried to carry one bass drummer and two snare drummers in the old days. Once in Green Bay, Wisconsin, a man says to me, 'I'm the best snare drummer in this state.' They're always the best, to hear them tell it.

"I told him bring his drum and we'd try him out in the grand entry. We put him in a fancy uniform for the walkaround. This guy had a deep Army drum and he insisted on carrying it low. It bounced on his knees so hard he rarely could hit the thing.

"But he managed to get around the hippodrome track and we went on the bandstand. He missed half the drum cues in the first two numbers. I told him to cease firing and watch the performance. We left him in Green Bay.

"Joe Simon came out of Jonesboro, Arkansas, and got his first job with an outfit called the Jewell Kelly Stock Company. Then he went on Happy Jack Morgan's Foot Train Circus. Later Joe was bit player and prop man with the Hickman-Bessey Stock Company. Next he was clarinetist on the Barnum & Bailey Circus, and then joined me as clarinetist on the big combine.

"As my librarian and the band's business manager until poor health forced him to quit in 1929, Joe had to keep track of 1,500 marches, 300 overtures, 200 operatic selections, 70 galops, 150 waltzes, 75 trombone smears, 30 suites, 50 ballets, and 100 or more descriptive numbers—any of which was apt to appear on the program. That gives an idea of circus music.

"After his health failed, Joe Simon went into the entertainment business in Memphis. We corresponded until he died in 1955. Joe was the kind of man we liked to have on the band in the old days. A good musician, Joe didn't smoke and never took a drink in his life.

"Now, I'll tell you about the elephants, or rather the 'Ballet of the Elephants.' It came along in 1942 and Igor Stravinsky wrote the music. Now, good elephant music is something with a solid beat—a march, one-step, schottische, fox-trot, waltz or cake-walk would be good.

"We had thirty-seven elephants at the time and Walter McClain, the head elephant man, told reporters he was to say the elephants liked the music Stravinsky wrote. But Walter says they 'didn't give a damn whether they worked to Stravinsky's music or not.' He said elephants work best to music with a strong beat, but he hadn't found any beat in Stravinsky's music.

"I sandwiched the Stravinsky music in between Weber's 'Invitation to the Waltz' and Ponchielli's 'Dance of the Hours.' We had to run those elephants in with music they knew or they'd never get started. And we had to get 'em out when their turn was over.

"The Stravinsky music was all chopped up—three-quarter time for two measures, two-four time of three measures, three-eight for five and so on. The cornet part was too high, the clarinet had more notes than anyone could blow. It took my boys quite a while to master it. Once we rehearsed for nine hours to play it three minutes. In all the years, I never memorized it.

"George Balanchine supervised the choreography and his wife, Vera Zorina, led the ballet. But the act never went over very big. It got so my boys in the band would mutter, 'Here comes Igor,' when the elephants' music cue approached. Then they'd say, 'There goes Igor,' when it was over, in a tone that meant 'We're glad that's over.'

"Let's just say it was Harvard music and let it go at that. It wasn't what the elephants needed, or deserved. But I understand Johnny North paid Stravinsky $1,500 to write it."

Merle recalls that certain numbers were taboo in certain parts of the country years ago, as far as circuses were concerned, just as "Dixie" was ruled out by many colleges and preparatory schools in recent years.

Changing times have reduced circus bands to less than two dozen (1968)

Never would the circus band play "Dixie" in certain cities years ago. Neither would it play "Marching Through Georgia" in that state.

But the classic came one time in Detroit, Michigan, and it still mystifies Merle. For the show's closing spectacle that season, which was a patriotic theme, Merle had chosen "The Star Spangled Banner." He was busy leading the band in our national anthem when a man from the crowd stepped up beside him and said with threatening emphasis:

"Mister, you can't play that song in Michigan. It's against the law. And if you ever play it again, at a circus, we'll put you in the penitentiary."

Ever since then, Merle made certain he ended all performances in Michigan with "Auld Lang Syne."

A typical program used by Merle and his circus band was made up after the circus equestrian director and band leader conferred and worked out a diagram and chart. The diagram showed three circles, each representing a ring, and two squares representing the stages between the rings.

Names of several performers appeared on the chart with a few cabalistic words explaining what those performers did. The chart was divided into 23 sections, each representing a display or number on the program.

The band leader then made up his musical program from this skeltonized bit of information, choosing numbers he thought best fitted the acts and actors.

If possible, he held two rehearsals of the band, then one dress rehearsal with performers. After that, he was ready for the opening and the show went on without a hitch. There might be a few slight changes, to meet conditions, but as a general rule the band gave out with the same slick musical numbers chosen in March for more than 450 performances in any given year.

21

Country Boy from Kansas

Merle Evans has always been fiercely proud of his home state of Kansas, his hometown of Columbus, and still calls himself "a country boy." During his travels around the country for more than sixty years he has had many happy meetings with fellow Kansans and greeted every one of them with boyish enthusiasm.

In spite of his busy schedule, he always found time to go home for a visit once or twice a year to visit his mother and other relatives and friends. Even after she died and his brothers and sisters moved to other cities, he never lost interest in Columbus and still goes back at least once a year, more often if he can.

Toward the end of her life, Merle's mother became hard of hearing so he had a hearing aid installed in the Presbyterian church so she could hear the music and sermons.

"After she passed away," he says, "the preacher asked me what he could do with the hearing aid. Well, I never was too much of a church-goer—just didn't seem to have the time or it wasn't convenient except when I was at Hardin Simmons. I went plenty there.

"So I says to the preacher, 'Give it to somebody else who can use it. I got no use for the thing.' And I guess that's what he did."

Merle is a director in the Columbus State Bank, run by his good friend, Bill Hamlett. The band master attends directors' meetings at least once a year, more often if possible, and at other times is represented by telephone calls or correspondence.

But he doesn't believe in putting all his eggs in one basket or all his money in one bank. He carries accounts with all the several banks in his adopted hometown of Sarasota, "so if one goes broke I won't get hurt too much."

Merle likes to tell the story of Had Babb, the town character of Columbus for many years.

"This Had Babb was a friend of mine; he liked me a lot. He was a fat old guy; always dirty. His hair was never combed and his old whiskers were matted. Oh, he was a mess. He was a great big fellow, always wore overalls with the bib.

"Old Had carried an enormous stomach; oh, it stuck out like a balloon, so he could hardly walk. It was terrible. And he lived in the worst old place—a house about twenty feet square with a pot-bellied stove; lived all alone in this dirty old house.

"Every time I went to Columbus, old Had would be waitin' for me, wantin' to see me. So I decided I'd do a big favor to old Had.

"I took him all over town trying to find something to hold this great big belly in; couldn't even find a corset in town big enough. So I took him to a tire shop and they got an old inner tube and cut it to make a sort of wide belt to hold Had's belly. Made him look a lot better, and he said he felt better. I can believe that.

"Every time I'd go home I'd fix old Had up. I'd take him to Tub and Skeet Whitcraft's barber shop for his yearly haircut and shave. Then I'd make him take a bath and I'd buy him a complete outfit—shoes, sox, underwear, shirts, cap and overalls; the whole works.

"Then Had and me would go rabbit hunting. Maybe Bill Hamlett would go along, too. We'd take my .410 gauge shotgun and a rifle and drive out through the country and shoot cottontails.

"I'd shoot 'em and Had would hop out and pick up these rabbits. Maybe we'd get twenty or thirty and he'd throw them in the car. Had would skin and clean these rabbits and we'd hang 'em on nails on the back porch overnight, so they'd freeze.

"They were wonderful eating. Oh, nothing like those tough old jackrabbits around Abilene. These were Kansas cottontails and good eating. We never ate those Texas jackrabbits.

"I'd always fix old Had up with groceries, too. I'd buy him bacon and eggs and butter; lay in a lot of canned goods. Then I'd take him to the overall factory in Columbus and they'd measure him.

"I told 'em when Bill Hamlett calls, make an outfit for this man. Old Had Babb thought a lot of me. He'd inquire when I was coming home and when I got there he'd be standing on the corner at the Columbus State Bank, waiting for me; old Had and his whiskers."

The late Ned Aitchison, one of the town's leading circus buffs for many years, said "Had worshipped Merle until the day he died." Aitchison added:

"Merle very seldom forgot a name and always had a good word for everyone he met. He always talked very fast and had a good story to tell. The big one will never be the same without Merle on the bandstand."

Honors poured in on Merle long before he retired from the circus. Governor Lawrence Wetherby made him a Kentucky Colonel and Columbus citizens held a banquet in his honor, followed by fireworks, on the town's 100th anniversary. Governor Robert B. Docking of Kansas was among those paying tribute.

As early as 1933, Ned and Helen Aitchison started building a model circus and collecting material for a Merle Evans circus museum in his hometown. Thousands of lithographs, pictures and programs were donated.

When it was formally accepted by the Circus Historical Society on August 3, 1962, more than 1,000 persons from every state in the union attended and heard a 32-piece band play some of Merle's favorite music. Johnnie Marietta provided popcorn from his wagon, built in 1889.

Many honors have come to the bandleader. Here is the first meeting of the Merle Evans Ring No. 32, Circus Model Builders in Columbus, Kansas, where Evans was born. Left to right: Ned Aitchison, Merle and Nena Evans, Earl Burnsworth, and Johnnie Marietta

The museum is still an attraction in Columbus and the town has recognized its most distinguished citizen with huge neon signs at all four entrances to the community. They read: "Columbus, home of Merle Evans, the Bandmaster."

Paul Van Pool and Harold Fields, two of his good friends, met with others in Joplin, Missouri, on December 17, 1938, to form the Merle Evans Tent No. 27, Circus Fans of America.

The Merle Evans Ring No. 32 of the Circus Model Builders was organized in his hometown on August 24, 1959, and he is the No. 1 honorary member of the Circus Model Builders, an international group to which only ten distinguished persons are named.

His adopted town of Sarasota, Florida, used December 10 and 11, 1968, to pay tribute with parades, banquets and speeches.

"I never thought I'd ever see anything like this," Merle said when a plaque was presented to him, inscribed, "To Merle Evans, who in his 47 years as circus musician has by his superior ability become one of the world's best known and most respected band leaders of all time."

The Dexter Fellows Tent, Circus Saints and Sinners Club of America, paid this tribute to Merle Evans and his band after the tragic fire in Hartford:

> "In acknowledgment of and in salute to your heroism. When fire struck the Ringling Brothers, Barnum and Bailey combined shows during the matinee performance of July 6, 1944, in the city of Hartford, Connecticut, you proved yourself worthy of the highest principles of the circus trouper by acting in a manner above and beyond the call of duty.
>
> "The members of Dexter Fellows Tent are proud to pay you this tribute."

The citation was signed by James J. Walker, president of the club, who for six years was New York City's mayor.

At the Mid-West National Band Clinic in Chicago on December 20, 1968, Merle became the first person to receive the Conn Award. He also was presented the wind and percussion award by the National Band Association of America.

The clinic concluded with Merle leading a 40-piece band playing circus music. A reporter called it "An historic change of pace," adding, "The bandmasters, professors, instructors, and deans of music savored each moment of this hour to remember. When the band concluded the finale, 'The Greatest Show on Earth,' applause continued for several minutes.

"Merle then announced he was going to ask Paul Yoder to conduct while the circusman joined in playing the exit march, 'Barnum & Bailey's Favorite.'

"The audience of more than 1,400 cried 'more, more,' and Merle finally ended the program with 'Symphonia,' explaining that would be the last number 'because we don't have any more music with us.' "

The International Musician, in its issue of June, 1952 said:

"Since he plays to an estimated 25,000 people a day, it is not too much to say Merle Evans has probably played to a larger number of actually-present persons than any other single performer in history."

One authority has estimated he entertained 165,120,000 circus fans from 1919 through 1969, not counting Shrine circuses and innumerable college and high school appearances plus tours in foreign lands. Certainly no other musician can touch that record.

Down through the years, many banquets in Merle's honor were held in the old Brooks Hotel, where he once worked as a second cook and bell hop and on which he later held a mortgage. One of Merle's regrets is that the ancient hotel is shuttered now and too decrepit to be useful.

"All I ever got out of that old hotel," he laments, "was a chamber pot!"

22

Bandmaster in Retirement

It was a wild, windy day in Utica, New York, when Merle Evans made his last appearance as band leader on the Ringling Bros. and Barnum & Bailey Combined Shows, November 30, 1969.

"Cold; Boy, it was cold that day, and windy! " he remembers. "We played 'Auld Lang Syne' as usual and they stopped the show and announced it was the last day of the season. Then we played the exit march—always called it 'The Chaser'—to get 'em out.

"They took a lot of pictures but there was nothing unusual. No announcement about it being my last stand after fifty years. Nobody thought it was. They still thought and hoped I'd be back.

"But I thought it was a good time to step down. I still think so. Things have changed so much. Nena and I have had good times together. She's been good for me and I've been good for her. And we've got a lot of things we want to do."

So Merle has time to visit with friends and do the things he wants to do, with no day-to-day trouping. He still keeps busy with Shrine circuses, leading college and high school bands all over the country, and making records. He is an honorary member of 28 Shrine clubs and holds more titles than he can recall off-hand, even with his fantastic memory.

He makes appointments by calling or writing friends, perhaps a band leader or outstanding citizen interested in promoting music.

"Dear Bill," he will write. "I have such-and-such a date open. I'll be glad to work with your band, lead it in concert, and give a little talk. See what you can line up and advise.

Your friend, Merle."

Back will come a letter or perhaps a telephone call. If the city is within a thousand miles and time permits, he and Nena will make the trip by car, otherwise he will fly. He arrives the day before the event, and leaves immediately after. Even now, he doesn't like to waste time.

One week he may be in Elgin, Illinois, and the next in Melbourne, Florida, or Beaver Dam, Wisconsin. He saves programs from all of them and some are single sheets with no specific state, so even he has a hard time remembering when he appeared with the Rochelle Township High School Band, Woodrow Wilson High Band, Brookfield High School Music Department or West Senior High School Band.

"Oh, I have plenty to do," he says. "I like to ride, like to drive and see the country. I have a lot of correspondence, a lot of band work. Most of my records are out of print, so I'm making more.

"Those five albums I cut for Crest last spring, they're my best, I had players from the New England Conservatory Wind Ensemble. They were remarkable. We played some old stuff that had never been recorded; some of it went back to 1872.

"You won't hear a flaw in these records. Everybody was right on the ball. I think the numbers they'll talk about most are 'Clownette,' a descriptive thing, and 'Honey Boy on Parade,' by Eddie Capiro. 'Radio Waves' is a very unusual march by Fred Jewell. He also wrote 'March High Mighty' for P. G. Lowrey, the greatest colored cornet player of his time. 'Fire Jump Galop' I wrote in the 1920s for Dorothy Herbert, who rode a horse over fire.

" 'Steeplechase Galop' was written by Russell Alexander many years ago. He was a baritone player and a good one. You'll hear 'Circus Kings,' which Charlie Duble wrote for Charlie Sparks. It was used on the Sparks shows for many years.

"Let me say I haven't missed the circus one iota, not one iota. Oh, we miss friends on the show and miss seeing a lot of people we used to meet along the way. But we keep in touch by letters and phone calls. I hear from band leaders and musicians all the time, a lot of them.

"But as far's the show is concerned, I haven't missed it at all. I like to do just what I'm doing now—visiting different places, giving talks, making some records. I manage to keep busy as ever."

There are no children or grandchildren to hinder their comings and goings. Actually, the Evans family is not close-knit and Merle has been away from his relatives most of his life. Recently a brother came from Kansas for a couple of days visit and after he left a sister arrived from California to spend a weekend on her first trip to Florida.

Merle and Nena recently bought a new home in Sherwood Estates, a typical Florida residential area of plush new homes on wide, curving streets with two-car garages and all the conveniences and luxuries of the 1970s.

They get out of bed shortly after 6 a.m., have a light breakfast and feed the birds in the big back yard. He'll read the paper, then drive into town to pick up his mail at the post office, where he always sees some old friends.

Back home, he answers many letters and makes phone calls, then has a light lunch, perhaps a sandwich and tea. If visitors drop in, he might drive with them to a restaurant for a snack and pleasant hour. He is friendly with everyone and always inquires about circus people in the area.

If need be, he may sort out some pictures, programs and music from his large collection, accumulated in sixty years of trouping in this country and abroad. The house sparkles with life-size paintings of Merle and banners bearing citations.

"I sent a lot of music up to the Museum of the Circus in Baraboo," he explains. "Some of it dated back to 1902. My music is in several museums. Freddie Daw down at Circus Hobby Hall in Coral Gables has some of it, and a lot of my souvenirs."

Merle, who still walks, talks, and thinks fast, watches his diet and tries to keep his weight around 185 pounds on his five-eleven frame. His reddish hair is thinning but his blue eyes still have that youthful sparkle and his step is quick and firm.

"I took Nena up to Mayos for a checkup," he says. "So I told them to look me over while I was there. They asked me, 'Who's your family doctor?' 'Family doctor,' I says. 'Why, I never had one. Never had a doctor in my life.'

"So they put me through all of these tests for two days. Finally, the doctor says to me, he says, 'You might as well get going. We can't find a thing wrong with you. Fact, according to your charts, you're a man half your age!' "

If there is a baseball game in town or nearby, Merle will be there. His favorite team is the Chicago White Sox, which holds spring training in Sarasota. He'll even drive to a nearby town to see a game.

"I love baseball," he admits. "I should have been a ballplayer. I like football and watch the games on TV but I don't understand all the finer points. In baseball, you can see what's going on; when a man gets a hit, steals a base, or makes a great play. Baseball's my dish.

"I never went in for golf, tennis, bowling, or any of those things. Never played much pool. I just never had time. I'd rather play cornet. And I didn't need the exercise—always got plenty of that leading the band."

He neither drinks nor smokes, but if friends drop in he will mix some daiquiris and serve them; might even sip one himself, just to be

A recent photograph of Nena and Merle Evans

sociable. There are always snacks on the table, and a big bowl of popcorn. He still loves popcorn.

Nena, the same age as her former boss, John Ringling North, worked for the Norths as secretary and bookkeeper on the show from the time she and Merle were married. Henry Ringling North, the younger brother, is one of her favorite people and she thinks he is "marvelous."

When the new owners, Irvin and Israel Feld and Judge Roy Hofheinz, took over the circus in November, 1967, Nena stayed on in the same capacity as before, retiring after the red and blue units left winter quarters at Venice for their 1970 tours.

To spend a day or a weekend with Merle and Nena is a delightfully refreshing experience, but to have an evening with them and their very good friend, Art Concello, is a rare privilege and a memorable occasion.

These two veteran troupers are like brothers and their quick wit and repartee keeps the conversation sparkling. It is something not only to see and hear but to feel in roaring laughter.

Concello, a born showman and recognized as one of the shrewdest circus operators of his time, was with the show except for brief interludes from 1930 until it was sold in 1967, first as triple somersault star of the flying trapeze and then as general manager, directing the entire operation with clocklike precision, making swift, positive decisions and keeping the show in the black.

In between times, he invented folding seat wagons which, in use, also convert to dressing rooms underneath. He fashioned new rigging for use in auditoriums and coliseums and made other improvements in circus equipment. Art is circus all the way.

He lives in a sprawling home a couple of miles from the Evans house. It is a bit more lavish, with swimming pool in the living room and just outside. The pool inside may be closed and heated in cold weather, and there's a tunnel connecting them so one may dive in from the living room and swim outside without taking a step.

"I didn't want people spying on me so I bought the land around here," Art explains in his soft, matter-of-fact way.

The house is surrounded by paved, curving driveways leading to streets on two sides. The nearest neighbors are outside shotgun range. There is a four-car garage attached to the house.

"He had it built this way," Merle says, "so he never has to back up. Art never backed up. Doors open automatically and he drives in. Then they close. When he starts out, they open and he goes forward.

"If Art wakes up any time day or night and wants to know the time, all he has to do is look at the ceiling in his bedroom. The time is reflected there. I don't know why he did that—he sleeps 'til noon! "

"Not always," says Art. "I get up when I want, or when I have to. No sense living any other way."

While driving around Sarasota, Merle will frequently call out, "There goes Art."

"You mean that was Art Concello we just passed?"

"Oh, no. Just one of his cabs. Art owns the cab company."

"The only reason I got the cab company," Art explains, "was I bought the building. This property down on Twelfth Street is a good location, five stores in it. And this guy says to me, 'You bought the building: I'm sick. I got these cabs and I wanta get out.'

"So I says, 'All right. I'll buy the cab company. So you can get out.' So I got the cabs."

Swing the conversation around to the circus—Art knows all about it for the last forty years, as intimately as Merle does.

"So what the hell are you doing now, writing a book on Merle I hear. I've seen the one on the Ringlings; very good. This Merle—that should be a snap. For Christ's sake, he must have a million pictures. Merle's the kind of guy who saves everything. He never threw anything away.

"Funny thing about Merle. He was with the band in all these towns, year after year. He had more goddam friends! Every town we'd go into, all these people would come around. 'Where's Merle? Where's Merle?' Everybody wanted to see Merle.

"Of course, Merle's situation is he wasn't like an actor. An actor works maybe five minutes, eight minutes or maybe even nine, and he's done. Merle's got to be standing there half an hour before the show. And he's there the last thing, too.

"Merle's a remarkable man for his age. Christ sake! Merle's—I don't know how old Merle is. He'll probably tell you he's fifty-two but he's closer to eighty if the truth was really known.

"Anyway, people would come in every town. 'Where's Merle Evans?' And I'd say, 'Well, he's around. He'll be here pretty soon.' And every night all of 'em has got something for Merle, a present—pie, cake, chicken, a whole damn ham. It's for Merle.

"Most of these gypsies, they'll say, 'It's good to see you; I'll see you next year,' and be gone. Not Merle. He'd stop and ask, 'How you been? How's the family?'

"He used to write every son-of-a-bitch and his brother, in green ink! I guess that's why they'd all come around, and bring something. We had a station wagon to take people to the trains after the show. And he'd chat a while and then say, 'Hey, that station wagon's waitin' for me. I'll see you. Goodbye.' He was always friendly, but never tied up with towners.

"The mailman would get a stack of mail every day, for Merle. That night or next morning, Merle would sit down and write letters, in green ink. He'd say 'I'll see you at such and such,' and name the date, or maybe 'I'm going to make a record; you be sure and get it.'

"Merle was always a workhorse. He doesn't know anything else. For years he was up there leading that band, getting his music together. He comes to me and he says, 'Hey, I want to go to Europe.' I says, 'All right, I'll send you to Europe. You get up there and lead the band a couple of days, then take off; go away.'

"I sent him to Europe and South America. Each time, after the show's set, I says to him, 'Go away. Get away from here. Forget the show. Have some fun.'

I'll tell you another thing: Merle is a helluva sports fan. Baseball, fights, that sort of thing. I remember one time the girls were doing a number with Merle. He wanted to be at the fight, but he's got to be on that stand. He's leading the band but he's watching the fight on television—I think it was Sugar Ray Robinson.

"Anyway, he's leading the band and watching this fight on a little TV off to one side. The girls are all looking and he was following the action, just going faster. So finally one of the girls comes over and says, 'Hey Merle!' " And he says, 'Oh,' and gets back to the music.

"He's been around forever; been around forever. Looks good. You see, Merle didn't have any bad habits; didn't smoke or drink, always got his rest, didn't dissipate in any way.

"Merle got the musicians, got 'em set and you could depend on him. He was standing there, ready. You never had to give it a thought with Merle. You knew he'd be there. He had a good drummer, Red Floyd. I noticed one season he wasn't there and I said, 'Where's the drummer?' He says, 'I fired him.' Next season I see he's back."

Art, would you say Merle is thrifty?

"No doubt about that; no doubt about that. He's closer than the paper on the wall."

Now it's Merle's turn to talk about his good friend and fellow trouper.

"Oh, Art's a good friend of ours, good friend. We visit back and forth quite often, like tonight. Art did a lot for Nena and me—sent me to Europe, Russia, South America. He paid us off in a lot of little ways like that. No money, you understand; just favors. Art wouldn't part with money. Oh, he's got plenty, but he won't give any of it away. Wouldn't give you the sleeves out of his vest!

"Art, you remember the time we had those posing statues? With costuming they'd be terrific. Mickey Graves' wife was on the show and she'd do a statue. She was flat-chested. Everything would show under these white tights, in this statue thing.

"So Mickey sent a fellow to the grocery store and told him get the biggest coconut you can buy. He sawed it in half, got the meat out and gave it to the workingmen. And he told Judy, 'Now, remember, these things will turn around and might slip down, so be careful how you twist your body. He smoothed them up and put these two half coconut shells up here, see?

"The girls posed as Indians at this water fountain and finally Fred Bradna got impatient and blew the whistle. He says, 'Hurry up, hurry up. Get out of here!' The girls had to move fast, and one of these coconuts dropped down. So one was to the north and one to the south, on Mickey's wife!

"Now if you two clowns will shut up for five minutes, I'll tell you how it really was," Nena says.

"I never had anything to do with the performance," begins this gritty, vivacious, and outspoken redhead, who can match words with any working stiff, and tell him off, but has a heart as soft as butter.

"My work was always in the office and my office was on the train. There was no glamor to it. Oh, some of our old press agents used to try to glamorize it, make a big thing out of it. They'd come around and say, 'What's glamorous about your job?'

"I'd say, 'Not a damn thing. There's nothing glamorous about it, nothing unusual. It'd just a job; like any other job in an office, only it's on the circus train.

"Once in a while some outsider would ask, 'When does the circus pay off? I mean what day, what time?' And I'd tell him, 'Every week, why?' I wouldn't tell 'em when, what day or whether night or day. It wasn't anybody's business.

"Oh, I'd get pressure from some of these so-called 'artistes' trying to find out what others got. They'd come around and say, 'Nena, I hear Sally is getting eight hundred a week. Is it true?'

"I'd say, 'None of your business. I'm not going to tell you what she or anybody else gets.' Or somebody would come along and say, 'You won't deny she's getting' three-fifty a week, will you?'

"I'd say, 'I'm not denying anything. It's none of your business.' Some of them would really get mad; they'd try every way to find out how much somebody was getting, but they never did."

Naturally, there was keen rivalry between performers and entire acts and these sometimes developed into towering jealousies which Merle and Nena always avoided. They are real troupers and have kept their friendships on and off the show.

"Oh, we have wonderful friends," Merle says. "I couldn't begin to name them all, even on the show; not even half of 'em. Some of them we've known for thirty years or more."

"I'll tell you exactly how the circus was," Nena said with an air of finality and authority. "Mr. Israel Feld, the show's executive vice president and treasurer, came into my office three weeks before the end of the 1969 season; came to see about some things, like any businessman.

"They were talking and he says, 'I guess Art Concello made a lot of money on the show.' I said, 'Mr. Feld, all our friends made a lot of money with the circus.'

"And that's the way it was. They made a lot of money and we had a lot of fun."

Epilogue

As "Gabriel of the Circus," Toscanini of the Big Top" and many other things in his more than 60 years as a musical entertainer, Merle Evans has become a legend in his lifetime.

As a man who has directed music for every type of public entertainment, he is recognized as the foremost bandmaster of the age.

The circus band has style and rhythm all its own, with a very fast tempo, exciting, thrilling, lifting the listener onto clouds of happiness.

The circus band is primarily brass, with an abundance of saxophones, clarinets, trombones, cornets, baritones, bass and snare drums and French horns. Drums are essential because they set the tempo, accentuate the tricks, and catch the falls.

But every instrument in the band is essential because the band is very strong on attack and accent, and must keep the audience's interest at high pitch throughout the performance.

As the leader of the Ringling Bros. and Barnum and Bailey Circus band for 50 exciting years, Merle Evans had his choice of the best circus musicians in the world.

He was asked to select, from them, his Hall of Fame circus band.

"These, I think, are the best musicians who have worked for me during the last 50 years," he said. "If they could be brought together—many have passed from the stage of life—this would be the best circus band ever assembled anywhere. How they could play a circus program!"

HALL OF FAME CIRCUS BAND

Merle Evans, Bandmaster
1919-1969

Picolo	Max Ring
E Flat Clarinet	Martin Hoexter
B Flat Clarinets	Everett Gavin, Howard Johnson, Neal Segard, Jimmy Austin, Buck Weaver, Bert Plowman, Harold Hanson, Tony Ramirez.
Cornets	Bill Kirkise, Frank Seavey, Phil Garkow, Frank Sering, Joe Steffan, Henry Kyes.
Horns	Paul Davis, Pete Staluppi, Burr Holmes, Pete Schmidt.
Baritones	Nobel Howard, John Horak.
Trombones	Lew Bader, Stanley Czerwinski, Charley Duble, Gene Miller.
Basses	Harvey Phillips, Johnny Evans, Bill Bell.
Drums	Ray Floyd, Ray Brownell, Roland Sherbundy.
Organ	Pete Heaton.